HEIR CONDITIONING AT OPEN COUNTRY

Russell Hunter

iUniverse, Inc.
Bloomington

Heir Conditioning at Open Country

iUniverse books may be ordered through booksellers or by contacting:

iUniverse
1663 Liberty Drive
Bloomington, IN 47403
www.iuniverse.com
1-800-Authors (1-800-288-4677)

ISBN: 978-1-4502-9105-7 (sc)
ISBN: 978-1-4502-9107-1 (hc)
ISBN: 978-1-4502-9106-4 (ebk)

Printed in the United States of America

iUniverse rev. date: 07/14/2011

To "Cousin Margy"

with much love

Contents

Acknowledgments

I want to begin by acknowledging John Weiskopf, with whom I made contact at a very noisy, crowded, and confusing book fair at UCLA, and who was kind enough, then and through further contacts, to assist me in threading my way through the sometimes confusing world of self-publishing. Equally helpful has been my former student Ginny Jenkins, who, via countless e-mails and in person, continued to encourage me to move *Heir Conditioning at Open Country* from the first draft, typed on an old Smith Corona upright typewriter, to the current draft produced on my home computer, and finally to a real book.

Second, I want to acknowledge Kathleen Cory, Town Clerk of Lewisboro, in Westchester County, New York, for her tireless efforts to identify the site in the town of South Salem, where Open Country stood. That search involved both visiting suspected sites and searching through town records that contained the chronicles of Open Country's ownership from about 1912 to my cousin's death in 1963.

Finally, I want to thank Allen Lavinger for his indefatigable editorial work in discovering "nits" that escaped my eyes in the final draft of *Open Country*.

Foreword

The events in this account are—all of them—true. They were created from the relics of a then-bygone era, from belongings and traditions that had long passed into history prior to that summer at Open Country.

The story is both tragic and uplifting. Tragic because my little cousin had, at the time of her death, lived in a world of absolute silence for almost seventy years. She had begun to lose her hearing in about 1881, when she was nine years old; by 1900 she was stone deaf, and she lived for almost seventy years in that world of utter silence. Uplifting because she remained active and productive all of her eighty-seven years of life, even getting a job making ship models for navy flyers to use in ship recognition during World War II.

When I was a child, "Cousin Margy" as I called her until I was well into my teens, was my favorite person at Open Country, the family estate; she never tired of letting me "help" collect eggs from laying hens, watch the estate staff milk the cows (and occasionally let me drink milk still warm from the cow), use the butter churn that made Open Country's butter, watch her feed the pigs, and do those other things that went with being a "gentleman farmer" in those far-off days.

Because of some family difficulties, I did not see Cousin Margaret for some ten years after I graduated from college, but finally, in 1959, I made contact with her and visited her in the little apartment over the garage where she had moved after she could no longer live in the Big House.

That contact led to her visits in Los Angeles. Never having traveled west of the Hudson River up to that time, she nonetheless had the courage to fly out to spend several weeks with me, sightseeing throughout Southern California—often alone by RTD bus and other public transportation when I was unavailable at work.

She never mentioned Open Country to me save to refer laughingly to its condition, and when, after she died, I discovered that I was to share its contents with two other cousins of hers, her gift came as a surprise. The following account details our struggles to deal with the contents of a twenty-nine-room house that had been shut up for twenty years and that had belonged to a family of pack rats.

CHAPTER 1

Camelot and Camelot Lost

Brilliant sunshine filtering through red and gold maple leaves that last day gave Open Country a cheerful air that it had not worn all summer. The driveway seemed to open up in the October sunlight, and even the ruins of the broad porches that hugged the house seemed less grim and forbidding.

My footsteps still echoed hollowly in the great central hall, but the room was bright with sunlight from the second-story clerestory windows in the gallery above, and the room even seemed to smell better because the musty odor that had plagued us all summer was gone. Some leftover trash from the sale the day before smoldered gently on the hearth, but, as I walked over to sweep a last remnant of embroidered linen into the embers, I noted that the place seemed tidy at last.

Strips of wallpaper might hang from the walls and bare laths show through the plaster, but Cousin Margaret's home was clean and ready for its new owner. Whereas she would have hated the idea of people invading her home for a public sale, at least she could have no quarrel with the way we left it.

Leaving the wide Dutch door open, I climbed the stairs for a final, solitary, personal farewell. As I turned on the landing to look

1

out at the magnificent maples and the broad view that gave the house its name, the full weight of our summer's burden hit me like a thunderbolt, and I started to weep. While my footsteps echoed through the bare and empty rooms, the tears flowed achingly from some limitless source within me, and my final sight of the rooms was blurred with tears as my sobs echoed my farewell through the emptiness of the deserted house.

It was not the ruin of Open Country I was saying farewell to, but the warm and vibrant home I had known in my childhood. Here was the Green Room, where I heard my first music, a scratched recording of the Magic Fire music from *Die Walküre* played on a Victrola with an enormous wooden horn. Here—Cousin Margaret's bedroom where, after she was forced to retreat to the servants' wing, I found her bed neatly made and turned down, the pair of red-and-gold embroidered slippers as carefully laid out as they had been when I had toured the house before my parents had died years before, a sign that she had not quite given in.

Here also was the bedroom where, after the 1929 Crash, the two sisters had tried futilely to wrest from my dying Cousin Henry enough of the family money to keep Cousin Margaret comfortable in her old age, and where Cousin Catherine herself had died a year later. Here, too, was the spot on the porch where I used to sit and admire Cousin Margaret's garden over tea while I heard the family tales I loved retold and my genealogy analyzed. I smelled again the midsummer fragrance of spiced peaches cooking in the kitchen under Cousin Catherine's watchful eye, and the flower room was perfumed anew with the smell of new-cut English lavender.

There was more to it, however, than simple childhood memories and their loss. I was crying both for my own childhood and for the loss of something deeper, something rooted in the distant past, even before my birth. It was a farewell to a dream, a sense of security that had slipped from me without my knowledge. It was essentially my parents' world, a world that had lived for me through their eyes, their values, and the stories that they had told me as a child.

They gave me their dream—one of stability, of safety, of (for them) secure social position. Of social duty as well, but duty willingly assumed in return for that position. I had romanticized it, but this did not make the farewell any less poignant. I rather imagine that loss of a dream and loss of reality have much in common.

I had, during that summer, returned to that earlier time and to its values. While I had helped dig out relics of the past, sought to deal with them, and sometimes fought over them, I had revisited that time not as a child, but as an adult, and I sensed deeply the Camelot world I had lost.

That was the major source of my grief. I had long since wept out my grief for my parents, my cousins, and the others with whom I had inhabited that past. It was the past itself—my personal dream—for which I grieved. I feel a reflection of that sadness as I write this.

I had a lot to cry about, and it did me good to get it out of my system. Presently, I cried myself out. My tour of the house was finished and my farewell complete; I stepped out through the French doors in the living room into the sunlit ruin of the garden.

The acrid odor of boxwood struck my nostrils, the only tangible remnant of all that had been there. The rest was gone: an era gone, the stability of my childhood gone, loves and lives passed from existence into memory, the gardens turned into jungle, the furnishings escaped from the prison of dead storage into the warmth of other homes. Standing there, smelling the boxwood and looking at the syringa bushes, I thought again of the sweet smell of their June blossoms when I had first returned to Open Country weeks before.

This is more than the story of that summer at Open Country, it is an allegory, a tale of Camelot and Camelot lost. It is also about a woman who would not give up and about the never-ending conflict between both the essential decency and the greed that are in us all.

The Open Country world of my youth was Camelot, a dream world of plenty and of leisure. It was a world in which some people, the fortunate, had leisure, leisure to appreciate the little things of life that appear to have been lost since that time—the sweet songs of birds, the scent of honeysuckle, the perfection of a dewdrop. And yet there was greed within that world—greed, ambition, and burning anger—a Mordred who leveled the walls about my deaf cousin's shoulders and set the stage for her final problems. There was, unfortunately, no Galahad to save her.

The allegory of Camelot fits that summer at Open Country as well as it does the demise of Open Country itself. For some of us brought Camelot with us to the dismantling of that dead world. While we dug out the relics of the past in our archeological dig, we lived in our own world of essential decency and gentility and attracted to us those who were like-minded. As in Camelot itself, however, there was a Morgan le Fey, and there was, in addition, a succession of Mordreds. That they did not succeed in their designs was due to the appearance at the last minute of a Galahad, a man who had the experience and humanity that we needed, who possessed those gentle qualities that we shared, and who was willing to pull our irons from the fire at the last minute.

This is, then, the story of the dream of Camelot, the perfect city that lives in us all; it is also the story of the greed that occasionally takes over that city from within or from without. It is, above all, a story of human beings with their strengths and their weaknesses.

CHAPTER 2

A Remarkable Woman, Your Cousin ...

It had all begun four months earlier, with the arrival in my West Coast home of a telegram from Cousin Margaret's lawyer.

> "Regret to inform you Margaret Leverich died Saturday. Funeral Tuesday at Greenwood Cemetery. Details to follow.
>
> John E. Quinn

I immediately felt a keen sense of loss. I had known my little cousin and her country home, Open Country, from the time I was a baby. This was the final loss of my childhood.

All of those who had known me in that childhood and my teen years—my grandparents, my parents, Cousin Margy's brother and sister—were gone. She was the last of them.

Though there had been an interruption in our relationship in previous years due to a family disagreement, I had reestablished contact with her a couple of years before; she had visited me on the West Coast two winters in a row and had thus become part of my present. Now she, too, was gone, definitively gone.

A few days later I received a letter from Mr. Quinn, giving

me the details he had promised, details that included the fact that my cousin wanted me to share the contents of her home, Open Country, with two other cousins whom I had not seen for thirty years. Although I appreciated her generosity, I wondered how much there might be for Lloyd, Katherine, and myself to share and whether the Big House was even safe to enter after years of neglect.

A few weeks later, I received a letter from Lloyd Robertson. He and his wife had visited the house shortly after my cousin's death.

"Katherine (his sister), Louise (his wife), and I know Cousin Margaret sold almost everything of value some years ago. Our mother bought a quantity of table silver, some chairs, and a bed or two, etc. Yet, I dare say, there is quite a job before us.

"The whole place seemed in pitiful condition. I can't bring myself to give many details. It was devilish cold, cold enough to see one's breath in the house all day. The large house is musty. Much evidence of water leaks, tattered wallpaper, crumbled plaster all about. Really disturbing when I recall former times. Quite happily, I report the furnishings are in passable order for the most part.

"I don't wonder Cousin M. didn't want you to enter the house (referring to an earlier letter of mine); I am sure she wouldn't have let us in either if she were alive. How horrible to see one's house go down that way."

Later in the spring I received another letter: "We returned from a visit to the Big House several days ago. Tired, but relieved in the knowledge that we have "licked" the servants' wing. Little enough indeed, but a step in the right direction. When I write licked the servants' wing, I mean separated the chaff from the chaff.

"Apparently, Cousin M. used that wing as a catchall for all the general and sundry oddments in that part of Westchester County. Don't think me critical; it is merely a statement of fact. We found nothing of value, only old clothes, letters, papers, and toilet effects.

Cousin M. also left a number of lists of things sold through antique dealers."

In May, after I had written that I would go east to help, he wrote again: "We'll all be glad to see you and have your help. There is still much to be done. Louise and I made our ninth trip to Open Country on Saturday. At last, we begin to see a little headway. A good deal of trash has been cleared away, but much more to come. Things are progressing more slowly than we all thought they would. With your arrival, we'll find more heart for the job."

I left for the East in June, expecting to be there for about two weeks. At a distance, it appeared that, indeed, nothing of real value remained at Open Country, that our main task would be to clear out the house, selling what little we could and throwing out the balance so that no purchaser of the property would be able to mock our cousin's pack rat habits. I felt that I owed it to my two cousins, Lloyd and Katherine, as well as to Cousin Margaret herself, to lend a hand in the task.

Some instinct made me want both to meet with Mr. Quinn privately and to pay an informal and very personal visit to the house before meeting my cousins. The first interview would give me a chance to learn some things from Mr. Quinn about my cousin that I had not known before, and a visit to the house alone would enable me to renew my acquaintanceship with the home in which I had first known my childhood playmate. I therefore fudged on the date of my arrival on the East Coast.

I arrived there in a driving northeaster and decided to postpone my visit to the house and to see Mr. Quinn first. I was staying with Tom and Dorli Bates, friends of mine from college, in nearby Wilton, and, rather than brave New York traffic in a driving rain, I elected to take the train. As the train rumbled through well-remembered towns, I began to think about my little cousin and about all the ways in which I had known her over the years.

Cousin Margaret was stone deaf when she died and had been so for some twenty years when she first held me in her arms. Indeed, she was already losing her hearing when my father was born in 1890. Born in 1876, she began to have hearing problems when she was nine; by 1900, she was totally deaf.

Cousin Margaret saw the transition from the horse-drawn pre-electric age to the age of television and outer space as well as those changes wrought by two world wars. She was born the year the telephone was invented, born into a world in which the utmost in speedy communication was the telegraph (delivered by boys on bicycles), used in metropolitan areas like New York for in-town messages by the well-to-do much as we use a cell phone today.

Messengers were summoned by a bell-pull in the house that activated a switch outside connected to the local telegraph office. The latter was an important selling point since it meant that "the electricity," something not yet trusted, was kept outside the house. Elsewhere, the telegraph usually signaled illness or death. Outside of the business world, the arrival of a telegram was a frightening event.

It was a time when most houses still relied on either candles or kerosene lamps, though a few in the big cities had gaslight; a world in which the fastest available transportation was the train, or "the cars" as trains were called. Stagecoach feeder lines existed for those who lived far from the railroad, much as buses today ferry passengers from airports to outlying districts. Horse-cars were the standard mode of public street transportation for those who had no carriages; the cable car, now only found in San Francisco, had just been invented but had not yet to found its way to the streets of New York.

In Cousin Margaret's youth, steam-powered elevated trains began to rattle above the New York streets, affording passengers a view of the unfortunate occupants of second- and third-floor apartments, scattering ashes on pedestrians below, and frightening the horses. In my own youth, trains still rattled above, but they were electric-powered. Almost all ocean-going ships were still made of wood and propelled by sail, though passenger vessels were driven by steam. A great deal of freight, indeed, was still carried in square-rigged and schooner ships until World War I.

Cousin Margaret saw the conquest of many of the diseases, such as typhoid fever and diphtheria, that had been dreaded household words in her youth. Even the cancer that carried off her sister and brother had become more controllable by the time of her death, if caught in time. Otherwise, the only parallel today is, for the most part, AIDS, though that is not now the killer it once was.

During her lifetime, Cousin Margaret saw the invention of incandescent electric light, the electric motor, the combustion engine, radio, the "flying machine," radar, and television. At the very end of her lifetime, man had invaded space, though she did not live to see the first man on the moon. Had she done so, she probably would have asked what good it might do.

Spiritually, however, she remained in that older world, a world of peace, comfort, and stability for her, even with her handicap. It seems possible to me that she may have clung to Open Country out of unwillingness to give up the last remnant of the world of her youth. It is a world now remembered by very few. I am acutely conscious of this because it was my world, too, and I find that few people understand, or are interested in, the world into which I was born.

Hers was the world rosily and lovingly described by Sir Winston Churchill as the "Sunset Age," a world that had not known major war for a hundred years in Europe, a time of peace, comfort, and tranquility for those with money and social position. (Sir Winston did not involve himself with the "lower orders," those who labored, cooked, and cleaned—and inhabited the appalling slums of London and the industrial Midlands.)

Servants were abundant, and the care lavished on the well-educated well-to-do gave them time to cultivate the arts of living. It was a leisured age, one in which people had time to devote to the amenities, to conversation and letter writing. Telephones were awkward instruments whose fidelity was poor, and "long distance" was reserved for major crises.

Much, if not most, communication was via the written word, and the era lives for us through letters preserved by families like my own, who saved rather than threw away material of that kind. Our current world does not afford such luxury. Who has time to write a long letter after a pressure-wracked day at some office, after a horrendous trip on the freeway, bus, or subway? Similarly, for that matter, when this morning's dishes await us in the sink on our return, and we find that we are at the end of the line for the laundry machine in our apartment house (if there is one)?

It was not until that summer at Open County, almost a hundred years after she was born, that I began to grasp the tragedy that had taken place. In my youth, the fact that Cousin Margy was deaf was a fact of life, something not to be questioned any more than I had questioned my Grandfather Russell's six-foot-four frame. Little things kept showing up during that summer that taught us the full extent of the loss she must have endured as, by degrees, she became more and more deaf.

We learned, for example, that she must have loved music when she was young, for we found stacks of pre-1900 concert and opera programs stored away in the Big House, each bearing critical comments in her handwriting. Her handwriting on these programs grew less frequent in the middle 1890s and finally ceased entirely. Those early years must have been hard on her, with her family attending musical events she could no longer enjoy.

The last sound she ever heard was made during the presidency of Theodore Roosevelt. The last music, the last spoken word, the last song of a bird, patter of rain, warning of approaching footsteps, or opening of a door behind her. She never heard ragtime or the melodies that George M. Cohan wrote to glorify the America of that simpler age. She never heard the jazz of the Charleston era or the tunes with which Tin Pan Alley enlivened America's great romp with prosperity in the 1920s.

She was never bothered by automobile horns, never heard the voice of Franklin Delano Roosevelt, never heard a radio play or used a telephone, never heard the strident voice of Adolf Hitler whipping his people into an evil frenzy. Nor did she ever hear Ed Murrow broadcasting from war-torn London, the stirring, if inaccurate, words of "Praise the Lord and Pass the Ammunition," nor the church bells telling our grateful nation that the promise of the bluebirds over the White Cliffs of Dover had been fulfilled.

She never owned a television set. She had not been able to enjoy theater since well before World War I and had enjoyed motion pictures only as long as they were silent (though, typically, she did enjoy *Snow White and the Seven Dwarfs*, with its intense visual imagery; of course, she had read the original and therefore could follow the events in the film without having to hear the voices).

She told me she liked the animals and the dwarfs but thought the humans poorly done, all except the witch—she'd liked both the early and late characterizations that Disney provided for that character. But, then again, the witch was portrayed as a caricature in the motion picture. With the exception of Snow White and the Prince, all the rest of the characters were drawn as cartoon-type figures rather than attempts to show real people.

There was too little of the visual on TV to appeal to her. She never, of course, heard Elvis Presley or the Midwestern accents of her beloved President Eisenhower. Nor did she ever hear the Beatles. This last may have been just as well. To one raised on the waltz, their music would have been dissonance indeed. Throughout those years, as she grew from a young woman to an old one, the world in which she had known sound vanished and was replaced by one whose values she did not understand—and probably would not have approved of if she had.

While her own childhood world was being obliterated by war, depression, and then by war again, while the society of her youth disappeared, she was deaf to all things great and small. She never heard the wind soughing through leaves, summer thunderclaps, or children's laughter. For more than 50 years she lived in a world of utter silence.

This may have been the key to her remarkable attitude toward the world and her place in it. While she clung to those things that formed her distant past, she retained a lively, childlike curiosity about the world around her, as I was to learn when she visited me on the West Coast. She must have lived an increasingly isolated life after the turn of the century, as her youth faded into middle age. By the time her mother, my Aunt Annie died in 1923, Cousin Margy was apparently a confirmed isolate whose joy lay in growing flowers and raising vegetables for use in the house.

And yet, she apparently adjusted, for when I learned of a new operation that could restore her hearing, I asked her, during one of her trips west, if she would like to take advantage of it, if she would like to be able to hear again. She thought for a minute before she replied. First, she said, "No." Then, after another moment of thought, she said wistfully "I would like to hear the sweet birds sing." I thought of that remark again when I saw the bird feeder outside her kitchen window in the little apartment above the hothouse later that summer.

Her eyes were her ears. She read lips with astonishing accuracy and could follow most conversations if the speaker was turned toward her. When in a group, her bright eyes shifted from face to face as she followed the conversation. She had trouble in a large group, however, because of her need to face the speaker and to have the speaker's face in the light. Her own speech came out in a peculiar cracked cackle that was partly due to old age and partly the result of her inability to hear her own voice and monitor the tones accurately. When she got tired, she used to place her hand on her throat so that she could judge the loudness of her speech by feeling the vibrations of her vocal cords.

She also knew two-handed sign language and taught me to use it when I was a child. She did not need it to supplement her lip-reading, but she and I used to have great fun on the New

York subway, I mouthing my own words silently to her, and she replying in sign language. We were both always keenly aware of, and amused by, the silent New Yorkers around us, much like two children playing tricks on adults. Which we were. This also helped me learn to spell at a very early age, though whether she realized this I do not know.

From the time I was a child, I learned always to get within range of her eyes to avoid startling her, though she seldom jumped if someone touched her unexpectedly. When she stayed with me on the West Coast, I rigged a light in her room with the cord plugged in outside the door so I could signal her visually when the guest room door was closed.

Shut away as she was behind her wall of silence, she must have developed a world of her own. Conversation, especially general conversation, was difficult if Cousin Margaret was to be included. My parents, from the time I was very small, had given me careful instruction about talking to her, and we always made a special effort to face her when we were speaking so she could see our lips, even when we were talking to someone else.

I doubt that her own family had been that considerate all the time. She must have spent many hours isolated while the conversation flowed around her. Most certainly, at Open Country, her gardening role was one that she could carry out without much communication with others. Very probably, it was this isolation that enabled her to conduct her life as she did during her final thirty years, long after the family structure at Open Country had melted away under the battering of the thirties.

As young women during the Spanish American War, Cousin Margaret and her sister, Catherine, had done volunteer work. Family papers unearthed that summer attested to their raising funds for "ice machines" for yellow-fever sufferers. This work led to involvement in the American Red Cross, work that both women continued up to and during World War I. Cousin Catherine remained active in the New York chapter of the American Red

Cross until the last months of her final illness in the thirties. Her work had been considered of sufficient importance for her to be invited to the White House by presidents Wilson, Harding, Coolidge, and Hoover.

Cousin Margaret, on the other hand, gradually withdrew from this kind of involvement and retired deep into a shell of isolation. Finally, at my father's urging, she interested herself in the Nitchie School for the Deaf and was active with the school until Cousin Catherine died and Margaret's financial world came crashing about her thin shoulders. It took work on my father's part, for she was reluctant to come out of her isolate shell. First she taught lip-reading as a volunteer. Then, later, she became more active, finally served as a member of the Board of Trustees, and helped support the school with donations. This continued until financial problems curtailed her activities.

During those pre-Depression years, Open Country was alive with people and with the work of their hands. Like all big houses of that day, it was an institution, fed by and feeding those who lived in it. Vegetable and flower gardens, chicken runs and pigsties, fields and cowsheds filled the house with produce and provided the gifts traditionally given to departing guests, whether picked that day from the garden or preserved months before.

Open Country was attuned to the passing of the seasons from the earliest spring, when crocuses poked their hardy little heads through the cold earth and sometimes a late snow as well, to late fall, when the last chrysanthemums were clipped from weathered stems just before the first frost, while shocks of cornstalks stood in the fields exposing the pumpkin vines they had concealed during the summer.

The household itself was geared to the out-of-doors, to the produce that flowed from the fields, to the beehives, and to the various animals and domestic birds that were kept on the estate. Only during the coldest winter months, when the driveway was packed with snow and the trees bare overhead, did the house slumber. It was an uneasy slumber, though, for staff were maintained during the winter so that the owners might visit on weekends when they chose to escape the sophistication of New York life and seek the rustic atmosphere that was their true milieu.

Inside, the house assumed a personality that varied according to the seasons. In the spring, daffodils brightened the rooms; May and June brought the sweet smell of lilacs, roses, and full double peonies, the last-named often snatched from the garden when the first thunderstorm threatened. July and August brought with them the smells and flavors of preserving.

Cousin Catherine and Mrs. Antoni, the household cook, were famous throughout the family for their spiced peaches, and that smell dominated the house in July and August, until it was replaced by the delicate odor of English lavender in September. Cousin Margaret tied the lavender in bunches and hung it on racks in upstairs bedrooms and placed it in every wall sconce in the house. The long autumns were dominated by the crisp smells of 'Mums and of wood fires in the sunken living room. I sometimes think of those today during our Los Angeles winters when the trees are bare and sometimes dripping with rain and the air is redolent with the smell of wood fires in nearby house and apartment fireplaces.

Cousin Margaret and Cousin Catherine had been brought up on a sugar plantation in Louisiana, and the love of productive country life was in their bones. By mutual agreement, Cousin Margaret had main charge of the gardens, livestock, and the flow of produce into the house; Cousin Catherine had charge of the kitchen. The former was generally quiet about her successes, but summer conversations with her forceful sister were dominated by the statistics of garden produce preserved in the kitchen where she and Mrs. Antoni presided over marathon canning sessions, so-called despite the fact that glass jars were always used in those days.

"Forty quarts of tomatoes this year," Cousin Catherine would observe in her booming voice as we sat around the living room

15

fireplace, "That's twelve more than last year." Her black eyes would gleam with satisfaction, her lips pursed as if she were savoring the preserves as she spoke.

They sold the produce they could not use themselves and were proud of the income it brought them, though it was no more than a hobby. Leftovers from that era that we found over the summer included rack upon rack of egg crates with wire cradles, dating from the days that Open Country sent eggs to market.

My earliest memories of Open Country belong to the halcyon years of its existence, an era of apparently limitless plenty. I first went to Open Country as a babe in arms in about 1924. I cannot remember it, of course, but family albums show me sitting on the grass in front of the house. My own earliest memory is that of music and goose grease.

I vaguely remember that the weather was cold, which means we must have gone there for a fall or spring weekend, probably going up to Katonah by train and being picked up by the chauffeur. I must have come down with a cold, for I have a mental snapshot of being given goose grease by the teaspoonful to quell a cough.

I also remember my mother telling me the story of the Magic Fire Music from *Die Walküre* and playing it for me on a Victrola with a huge wooden horn, so named because it was put out by the Victor Talking Machine Company of the attentive dog and "His Master's Voice" fame. I believe it was the first music I ever heard, for it was about 1927, and we had neither a radio nor a Victrola—or any other form of gramophone—at home in the city.

Like Kleenex and Xerox today, the name Victrola entered the lexicon of its time and was used to describe any music-reproducing machine in those pre-electric days. The word "gramophone," then so commonly used, has disappeared and is memorialized only in the Grammy Awards given out each year. Victrolas were expensive, and it was an era when most people listened to music live or not at all.

This was the world that I was born into in 1924. The stock

market was riding high, and Cousin Margaret, her sister, Catherine, and their brother, Henry, had moved from Queens in 1921, where the family had lived for generations, and taken up residence in Westchester County. If she thought about it all, which seems doubtful to me, it must have looked to her as if there would be no end to the plenty for my three cousins; that there would be no end to the halcyon life that they enjoyed before the Crash that would forever write *finis* to many prewar social structures both in Britain and in the United States.

Open Country was a wonderful place for me then. There were horses, cattle, and pigs, and a huge garden ringed with crabapple trees that were wonderful for climbing. The estate produced its own milk, and there were always pans of milk set aside for the cream to rise, as well as a hand-operated wooden butter churn to watch.

There were hens, setting and otherwise, and I have an uncomfortable memory of letting the chickens out of their run one day, to Cousin Catherine's anger and disgust. I can still remember that giant of a woman lumbering across the lawn bellowing about "Whoever let the chickens out," and being terrified. I now think that she knew I had done it, though she did not ask me. I would probably have been too frightened to answer. Perhaps she saw my face and, with a sensitivity unusual for her, decided I had "Learned My Lesson." Most certainly I never let them out again.

There was also a flock of geese that used to run free about the place, but they generally stayed close to the overseer's house at the end of the gardens. One of my few unhappy memories of Open Country is being chased, screaming, into the house by those creatures.

The kitchen was a place of wonder with its huge wood-fired range (which must have been dreadfully uncomfortable in summer) and all kinds of wonderful things always being prepared. Tea was served regularly at 4:00 p.m., and I can still taste the currant-flavored butter tea cake Mrs. Antoni used to make. The dried currants were, of course, Open Country produce.

After dinner and a final visit in the living room, when we went out to the car for the trip back to our own summer house, there would always be a peach basket filled with flowers and vegetables for us to take back home. Sometimes there would also be preserves, orange marmalade made from imported Seville oranges, spiced currants, or perhaps a comb of buckwheat honey. In the winter, our doorbell would ring from time to time in our New York apartment, and Frank Allmond, the estate overseer, would call up the shaft to announce that he was sending up produce from Open Country: farm-fresh milk, eggs laid that morning, or some of summer's largesse in terms of jars of tomatoes, beans, or new peas.

Open Country lay about five miles away from our own country home, Lacey Green, and I always looked forward to visits there, chiefly because of Cousin Margy. An only child, I was brought up on the principle that "Children should be seen and not heard." This was sometimes true at home and always when visiting friends and relatives. Cousin Margy was different. Possibly because her deafness isolated her from much that went on around her, she retained a childlike attitude about the world around her, an attitude that endeared her to me when I was yet very small.

My little cousin (when I was an adult she was a good head shorter than I) was my favorite person in the household. She was bright, with mischievous blue eyes and an elfin, cheerful personality. To the end of her life, she moved quickly and energetically, even though in her last years she was bent by arthritis. "I'll be walking on my nose soon," she used to say and then laugh in her high thin cackle. Without ever seeming childish, she took a childlike delight in the world around her to the end of her days. To that end, she maintained a genuine innocence and lived in a creative world that was uniquely her own.

She loved to garden, and spent hours doing the light picking and pruning she had the strength to do. The flower room was her province alone. At all times of the day, she could be found in the little flower room off the hall leading to the living room, humming tunelessly to herself and brushing back the wisps of hair that escaped her men's gardening hat.

She dressed very plainly in black buttoned shoes, utterly styleless cotton or wool dresses, and either a plain felt hat or a porkpie panama straw hat with a plain black band around it. She wore no makeup and dressed her silvery gray hair in an in an old-fashioned bun on top of her head, usually held in place by a black, elasticized band of ribbed silk. When working in the garden, she held her hair in place with a shoestring; when she dressed for a special occasion, she used a black velvet band for the same purpose. She had a special affinity for children, seeing the world through a child's eyes to the end of her life, and, if my experience with her is any criterion, she had an instinctive understanding what children liked and wanted.

She was always happy to have me share her world, whether outside or in the house. She let me "help" her in the garden, and we fed the chickens together. Sometimes she let me gather eggs, but only under her supervision lest I break them or disturb a "broody" hen. She fed me milk yet warm from the cow and let me taste sweet butter just out of the churn. We would visit the pigpens together, but she warned me never to go inside for fear I would be trampled on. Pigs can be very dangerous animals.

On rainy days when we could not go outside, she used to take me to the attic and tell me family stories about the things in the rows of trunks up there.

"This was your great-great-grandfather's policeman's badge," she would say as we browsed through one of the trunks. "He belonged to the New York Volunteer Police Department, rather like the Volunteer Fire Departments in South Salem and Ridgefield today." I knew what she was talking about, because we would hear the Ridgefield town siren go off every now and then and know there was a fire somewhere. If we were in town at the time, we would find that every shop or business was immediately denuded of help because a large percentage of the town businessmen were volunteer firemen and they would leave immediately to fight the fire.

Or, opening another trunk, "Mother, Catherine, and I bought this soap in Paris in 1894. And this wedding dress was worn by your great-great-grandmother Schuchardt," and so on. One package that used to fascinate me contained a wool dress belonging to Cousin Margaret's mother that had been packed in red pepper against moths. I used to wish that she would open it up so I could see if the pepper really worked, but it was sewn up carefully in unbleached muslin, and she never did open it up.

Whatever we did together, Cousin Margaret always shared with me riddles and sayings from her childhood that seemed to delight her as much then as they must have when she first heard them.

"Why does a steam locomotive chew tobacco?" she would ask.

"I don't know, Cousin Margy."

"Chew-chew to go ahead, and chew-chew to back'er!"

And she would go off into gales of cackling laughter at the pun.

She also taught me the following nursery rhyme when I was very small:

There was a little girl
Who had a little curl
Right in the middle of her forehead.

And when she was good, she was very, very good
And when she was bad, she was horrid.

When I bought my first sailboat with auxiliary power, I nicknamed its engine "Little Girl." As any sailing yachtsman knows, when marine engines are bad, they are horrid indeed.

They tend to be nasty, smelly, dirty things that break down at the most inopportune moments, generally at night and at sea. If they break down dockside, then the breakdown occurs at a time when a mechanic cannot be had for love or money because it is a long weekend.

This was the picture of my cousin that I carried from my childhood to my youth and young manhood, and finally through her visits to my West Coast home after my mother died. Between my childhood and adulthood, the Depression and my cousins' deaths took their toll of the halcyon life of former years. An entire lifestyle withered away, and the Big House began its slow decline.

Death did not come swiftly to it. As so often happens, the events that signaled its destruction had little effect at first. The stock market crashed, and the raids of Margy's brother Henry's on the family fortune appeared to have no effect on the permanence that was Open Country. Flowers, garden vegetables, and other produce flowed into the house as before. Mrs. Antoni's meals remained as superb as ever, and the inhabitants continued upon their normal rounds.

It was the Open Country of these years that I remember best, a household that had already received a mortal wound but continued on its way from its own momentum, very much like the *Titanic*, which remained a functioning entity, lights, heat, and the short-wave radio used for her SOS calls continuing to provide their essential services, and some passengers playing a customary card game, while the waters of the cold North Atlantic poured into the hull many decks below.

Six or seven years after the Crash, there appeared to be no change in Open Country. Silver and crystal graced the table, Cousin Margaret's style of entertaining had not changed, and Charley Antoni was always at the porch steps with a basket of produce or a box of preserves when we came to leave.

The thirties were, however, an accumulating disaster for Cousin Margaret, one that accelerated through the 1940s and 1950s. Their mother, my aunt Annie, had died in 1923 of a heart attack while she was putting her customary whipped cream in her coffee. She collapsed over the breakfast dishes and died on the spot. Her estate was never settled, a failure that was to prove fatal for the family.

Neither Cousin Margaret nor Cousin Catherine paid particular attention to their investments, while Cousin Henry, in defiance of an agreement they had made, dipped into the estate without informing his sisters. This did not create problems during the halcyon days of the middle and late twenties, for there always was enough to go around.

As the country slid toward the financial deeps of 1931, though, Cousin Henry had increasing difficulty in concealing either his losses or the extent to which he had robbed his sisters. Shortly after 1934, he contracted cancer, and it was during this illness that his peculations came to light. By this time, Cousin Catherine knew that she, too, was dying of cancer, and that her baby sister both lacked the wherewithal to live and the ability to support herself.

As soon as she realized the extent of the problem, Cousin Catherine took desperate steps to protect her deaf sister. She first shut Cousin Jessie (Henry's wife) out of the ground-floor bedroom where Cousin Henry lay dying and where she herself was also to die. Pompadour quivering and black eyes flashing with rage, dragging Cousin Margaret with her, she stormed in to confront him with their knowledge of the disaster he had brought upon them. My Cousin Catherine had the build, the forcefulness, and occasionally the voice of a bull elephant. My Cousin Margaret might have been unable to hear, but this disability apparently had had no effect on her vocal cords.

As the quarrel grew in pitch and volume, the entire household (the servants told my parents later) was privy to the demands that the two women were making of their dying brother. At tea time, they were still at it, and I rather imagine that Cousin Jessie had little appetite for Mrs. Antoni's butter cake (for it would have been unthinkable for tea not to be served on time).

As the afternoon lengthened into evening, they were still at it. It was not until Mrs. Antoni appeared at the bedroom door to announce dinner that it was all over. It was a bitter triumph, however, for there was not nearly enough of their mother's original million-dollar estate to support Cousin Margaret in anything like the style to which she was accustomed. Cousin Henry had agreed to sign over virtually all his money to a lifetime trust to be managed by Cousin Margaret, and his wife was all but beggared; Cousin Margaret paid her a small stipend out of the trust.

Cousin Henry died in 1933, and Cousin Catherine somewhat later. From then, the house slipped swiftly into its long decline. During the early part of this process, few changes were evident. If a few rooms appeared closed, that seemed only natural. Cousin Henry had died. His widow lived elsewhere, and Cousin Catherine was dead as well. A single woman living alone, Cousin Margaret would have been foolish to pay for upkeep on unused rooms.

Little by little, staff disappeared. First, household staff, and then the overseer. Gardeners were dismissed. Prices rose and Cousin Margaret's resources dwindled. As time went by, she rented out the chauffeur's apartment over the garages, the cars having long since gone. She also rented out the overseer's house on the back of the property, and she began to sell small parcels of land. One could trace these sales by the appearance of new houses built along the graveled country road on which Open Country stood. In addition, she put the Big House up for sale but placed an impossibly high price on it despite competent advice to the contrary. She probably had no real desire to sell. Little was sold from the furnishings of the Big House and that, typically, was sold to family.

The accumulated stress had its effect on the household, producing events that would have been unthinkable a few years earlier. It must have been a rare household as the war began, as revealed by a story one of Cousin Margaret's tenants told me about his and his wife's first dinner with her.

"They'd had a fight that day, Miss Margaret and Mrs. Antoni. I think it was about money. When Mrs. Antoni came into the living room to announce dinner, she was barefoot and wore an old cotton dress, her hair hanging down her back.

"Your cousin never turned a hair. She nodded as casually as if Mrs. Antoni had been wearing her customary black uniform with a white lace apron and led us into dinner. It was quite an experience. We ate a superb dinner by candlelight off your cousin's crystal, Spode, and old silver while Mrs. Antoni's bare feet slapped the floor as she served. Mrs. Antoni apologized to me about it later, but Miss Margaret never mentioned it."

It was during this period that the greatest changes took place. Cousin Margaret could no longer pay Charley and Mrs. Antoni, so they quit and retired to Bridgeport to open a restaurant. We envied their customers. Matt, the last remaining gardener, also left, but remained close enough to come and work for Miss Margaret from time to time, chiefly in the garden and in the woods. She had extensive woodlands, and she used to hire him to cut and split timber to use in the big kitchen range and later to fuel the laundry room stove. It was probably more expensive than buying coal, but the instinct to live off the land must have been strong in her.

I did not know this period at Open Country well. Cousin Margaret moved into the servants' wing while I was in the army during the war, closing the main and bedroom wings completely. I corresponded with my little cousin from overseas, of course, but the personal contact was gone. After the war, some difference of opinion between Cousin Margaret and my mother created a rift so that I did not see her with any regularity when I got back, and finally, I did not see her at all. She did, however, show up at my father's funeral with a twig of a tropical plant from her greenhouse that she asked be placed on his coffin. It was.

Up to the time of her death, she continued to sell items from the house but, as we were to discover, things with little real value. She made no real attempt to provide for her own comfort by selling the genuinely valuable items and investing or spending the proceeds.

It was during the war that she had her first and only real paying job. A cottage industry had grown up in the small town of Poundridge, about five miles away—one that involved the manufacture of miniature ship models for the US Navy to use in teaching ship recognition to its flyers. Somehow, Cousin Margaret learned of the project and worked there for about five years. She used to walk down to the main road, about a mile and a half from Open Country, and take the bus from there to Poundridge, returning in the evening. Even in good weather, it was a substantial walk.

Neighbors told me much later that not even a winter snow would keep her from her job. She, then in her late fifties, wrapped gunnysacks around her shoes and trudged through sometimes knee-high snow to the main road if the snowplow had not yet come through. In the evening, she would return the same way in the dark.

That courage, that persistence, was very much a part of her character. I rather imagine that the outlet was wonderful for her, though I do not know how much she was able to talk to people at work. She and I never discussed it. Of course, the money she made must have been welcome, though probably no more than a drop in the deep bucket of Open Country's needs.

She never mentioned this either, but I suspect that part of her reward was that she was making a contribution to the war effort, something important to almost everyone in those days. Most certainly, she tried in other ways, for example, through saving paper and tin cans, even though she apparently never had them picked up, or at least never had the last lot picked up. We found a substantial number of them in the house that summer, the newspapers tied in bundles, the cans neatly flattened and stored in cardboard boxes ready to be picked up.

After the war, she went on unemployment, as she had every right to do, and remained on unemployment as long as she was able. The family, typically, made snide remarks about it. That she was willing to make the effort to get to the unemployment office was, I think, a measure of her financial need. The family, of course, had no understanding of the depths to which she had been reduced by that time. Certainly I did not.

After that, Cousin Margaret did not work again. She appeared briefly at my father's funeral, but I did not see her again for years after that. My first contact with her was when I came east for my mother's funeral. I had long felt a tug to see her again, and my mother's death removed any obstacle to my picking up the threads of our relationship. On one of my trips east regarding my mother's estate, I wrote to my childhood playmate and asked if I might visit her. Also by letter, she agreed.

Cousin Margaret was established cozily in the former chauffeur's apartment over the garage. It was small and contained a living room, bedroom, and kitchen only. It was furnished with some antiques that had been brought over from the Big House, but Cousin Margaret's real pride was a small bird feeder outside the kitchen window where she could watch her little friends enjoying her largesse.

It was a strange visit, depressing but for Cousin Margaret's cheerfulness amid the ruins around her. She had shrunk with age, and her hair was white, but otherwise she was much as I remembered her from my childhood, the same cheerful, wrinkled, gnomelike figure with a shrill voice and the happy laugh of a child.

She gave me a simple lunch of fried chicken and green beans that had been frozen the previous summer as we tentatively became reacquainted with one another. It was not until after she died that I learned that she did her freezing using the waxed cardboard boxes that her one-pound butter purchases came in as freezer containers. Whenever she shopped for butter, she bought only a quarter-pound at a time, always, however, insisting on taking the entire original container when she left the store.

Each year, she rented space in the neighbors' freezer for her produce, walking down to their house when she needed something.

She thus maintained Open Country's tradition of self-support, which must have given her satisfaction. Either she reused the containers or she ate a great deal of butter, for I was to find a substantial supply of those containers in the kitchen at Open Country on my first day there.

After lunch, at my request, she took me over to the Big House. The house had looked grim enough as I drove up the driveway, but what I saw up close was worse, much worse. It had not been painted for twenty years or more. The shingles were curled, the shutters askew, and the gracious porch that circled the front of the house was a dismal ruin, its once-graceful columns replaced by unpainted two-by-fours looking very out of place but clearly necessary to support the porch roof. The Big House had become a Charles Addams cartoon caricature rendition of its former stately glory.

I asked about the inside, and Cousin Margaret laughed and said that it was a total ruin. Her laughing dismissal of my question forestalled any sympathetic overtures on my part, and also told me she had no intention of letting me see the inside for myself. As with so many other things in her life, I realized that she could only accept the ruin of her old home by laughing about it.

We returned to the vegetable garden, and she proudly showed me neatly weeded rows of carrots, beets, peas, and beans and tidy hills of cucumber and squash. Every spring, she said, Matt came over to dig up the garden for her and get it started. Thereafter, she did all the weeding, harvesting and freezing the things she did not use for herself. She sent me on my way with a jar of her marmalade.

When I returned to the West Coast, I thought about her a great deal. I thought about her enough that I resolved to invite her west the following winter. In a sense, I suppose I wanted to make up for all the years I had not seen her. In any case, never expecting that she would accept, I invited her to fly out for a visit the following March.

I picked March because I remembered that it is a difficult month in the east. Winter is very old by that time. Spring, while hoped for, is not yet just around the corner. I never expected her to accept because I knew she had never flown (she was then eighty-four years old), that she had never traveled further west than the Eastern Seaboard, and had not traveled at all, to my knowledge, for at least thirty-five years.

At first, she refused to leave Open Country. There were too many problems, she said. We corresponded about it for several months, and finally I simply sent her a plane ticket for a date that was three weeks away. She wailed, by letter, that she couldn't possibly make the deadline, hinted at the necessity of revamping her entire wardrobe, but she made the plane. It was to be the first of a series of late winter visits that we both thoroughly enjoyed.

When she first arrived, she was wearing the same hat I had seen her wear twenty years before, an absurd creation of blue felt, with perky little bows that had always reminded me of rabbits' ears. With it, she wore the same dark blue overcoat that she always wore "for good." She had never cut her hair short, of course, and kept it in a bun either at the back of her neck or on top of her head. Wisps of hair were forever sneaking out, and she was always tucking stray strands of hair under her hat.

During much of her stay with me, she wore dresses of fine lawn, stout laced black shoes, and a hat made of real panama straw (she was proud of the fact that it wouldn't crush) bound with a black grosgrain ribbon. This attire was in sharp contrast to the Southern Californians around her, a contrast sharpened when she visited Palm Springs.

On her arrival, she waved a cheerful good-bye to the stewardess at the plane door, and paddled happily down the steps bearing a wicker carryall bought in the Holy Land in 1909 (she told me), into which she had put a store of her ubiquitous and always welcome orange marmalade.

She brought with her a tremendous store of both curiosity

and energy. Each day, she wanted to go someplace new and to do something she had not done before. It was not until her final trip, a year before she died, that she rested for a day between sightseeing excursions.

She was a delightful guest and an exasperating one, independent and active and determined to make every minute of her visit count. Announcing the first night that she would do no cooking, she nonetheless stood at my elbow every minute I was at the stove, asking questions.

"What's that for?" greeted every new ingredient, and I would have to stop and explain. This meant that I had to shift my position so that the light fell on my face when I talked. I soon became adept at stirring things on the stove without looking at them. My sloppy bachelor habit of draining dishes in the dish rack after the "washing up" was not acceptable, and she insisted on drying everything after every meal.

I also found out that she was a saver, though the discovery did little to prepare me for Open Country. Not a paper bag or a piece of string could find its way into the trash while she was with us. "Save that bag," "Save that string," would be the cry whenever I thought I was not observed and tried to sneak something into the trash. She stayed three weeks each time she came, and, by the time she left, I had a whole drawerful of paper bags and string.

She had the curiosity of a child and a child's delight in seeing new things. An inveterate sightseer, she was not afraid to use public transportation. She expected me to provide her with something new to do each day, and each morning I would phone the Metropolitan Transit Authority for bus numbers and schedules on the route she was to follow. I dropped her off at the bus on my way to work, and she would vanish on the day's journey, finding her way back in the afternoon.

Eager as a child let loose in a toy shop, she saw and did everything within reach of Los Angeles. When she had exhausted the possibilities of the Metropolitan Transit Authority, she embraced

Tanner and Greyhound buses, venturing to Los Angeles Harbor, to Santa Barbara, to the mountains, and to the desert, almost always alone, meeting and chatting with people as she went.

Occasionally, the phone rang after I got home from work, and I would hear a slightly puzzled voice on the other end:

"I'm at the main MTA terminal downtown. Your cousin is here and she wants me to tell you that she will be home in a little while and not to worry about her. She is taking the 94 that passes your house at 6:37." If the call was more complex, I would hear her squawking in the background while her messages were relayed. I always wondered how she managed to collar them. I wondered with equal frequency what tales they had to tell of a little old lady who could not use the telephone because she was deaf.

Her sense of values was peculiarly her own, a product of her isolation at Open Country and from the spoken word. Her values were at once rural and cosmopolitan—and frequently out of date. Though she had lived in her rural surroundings for thirty-odd years, save for occasional trips to New York, she kept up-to-date with the world by reading the *New York Times* daily. She also did so on her visits with me despite the difficulty of getting it on the West Coast at that time.

She remained a Democrat of the Al Smith school and voted faithfully for Roosevelt, Truman, Stevenson, and Kennedy without really approving of them. Among first ladies, only Bess Truman was as retiring as she thought a president's wife should be. She granted grudging approval of Jackie Kennedy's work, though she made it plain that she wished she could do it with less publicity.

In my home, she always turned out the lights whenever she left the room, and carried this sense of thrift when she took a tour of CBS Television City arranged by my lover, who was in public relations.

"Tell me, young man," she asked the guide when he told her the number of electric light bulbs used to light the largest sound stage, "What is your electric bill here? It must be enormous." Thereafter, he told John later, she made him turn off all the lights as they left each sound stage.

Taken to a motion picture set, she was fascinated by the array of technical equipment and the illusion that was achieved. Her observation did not fail her, however. The show was *Private Secretary*, and the star, Ann Sothern, was being difficult that day and kept everybody waiting.

When Miss Sothern finally appeared and flounced across the sound stage, Cousin Margaret watched her dispassionately and then remarked, "I don't think I like her. She thinks she's better than other people." There was a ripple of laughter around us which, fortunately, did not carry far, given the state of Miss Sothern's temper.

The Brown Derby in Hollywood was a bust. She was not a moviegoer, and was unimpressed by the current crop of TV and movie stars lunching there. Grauman's Chinese Theater was more successful. She happily padded about, looking for the footprints of the stars of the silent era and the perennial favorites she had read about in the *Times* for years.

Forest Lawn was not for her. When she was shown the Columbarium, where the "Dear Departed" are encased in urns above ground, she was less than pleased. Stamping her sensibly clad foot on the turf, she announced, "Not for me. I want to be buried under the green grass." Happily, she was, in a cemetery with the engaging name of Greenwood.

She took a day trip to Palm Springs, the apotheosis of Southern California living, traveling in her lawn "summer dress" with full sleeves, black leather laced shoes, and porkpie hat. She returned spluttering.

"I don't know which is worse," she said, gesturing helplessly, her voice cracking as it always did when she was emphasizing a point. "What the men wore," a pause, "Or what the women didn't! And the clothes that the people did wear were awful!" Altogether, that visit was not a success.

The next visit to the desert was more successful. She and I drove down to see the desert in bloom, and we had been fortunate enough to have a wet winter. The only time when the East Coast competes with the brilliance of springtime West Coast desert color is in late summer, when whole fields will be yellow with goldenrod. When we got there, desert blooms carpeted the ground, providing a riot of colors and softening the harshness of the rocks and sand that dominate that landscape and make it, for me, too sharp around the edges for comfort most of the year.

Just as I do, she reveled in the bright colors. From time to time, we would stop, and she would be down on her hands and knees with a magnifying glass studying the "belly-plants," tiny plants so-called because one has to lie down on one's stomach to see them. She was fascinated by their microscopic perfection.

She was never happier than when she was studying flowers and plants. She examined my own garden exhaustively, wanting to know about every plant she did not recognize, necessitating several prompt quick studies on my part. She was equally curious when she went to the various arboreta in Los Angeles (she visited them all). Each time she came to visit me, we went to Descanso Gardens for the camellia and azalea exhibition, and she spent entire days at the Los Angeles County Arboretum and Ferndell.

When she left, I sent packets of succulents east with her, and after her death found them doing well in her greenhouse. During that final summer at Open Country, my cousins and I felt compelled to find homes for these and her other plants. We could not bear to leave them in the greenhouse to die. She had sacrificed too much to nurture them.

Certain little events during her visits stick with me and give me pleasure even today, more than fifty years later. One of these very pleasant episodes occurred during one of our desert excursions and impressed me because of the essential decency shown her. We had driven down to the Salton Sea and were having dinner before returning home. As usual, I had had to explain to our waiter that he would have to face my cousin and speak slowly so that she could understand him.

While we were waiting for our dinner to come, we continued to talk. Because the place was dark, I held the table candle to my face so that she could see. As I did so, I noticed that some member of the staff was gradually turning the lights up in the room so that she could see my lips better.

On that same trip, I discovered how difficult it was to drive with Cousin Margaret at night. I had to turn the map light on so that she could see—and then turn from the road so that she could read my lips. Not the safest or most comfortable of trips.

She toured Disneyland every time she came out, making the shrewd observation on her first visit, "Grownups have more fun here than do the children." Nonetheless, she made friends with every child she saw, and I found that she had lost none of her ability to make friends with them. Only a few were too surprised by her wrinkled face and bent figure to recognize and respond to the twinkle in her bright eyes.

She took the long bus trip to the Huntington Library, where she saw Sir Joshua Reynolds' *Blue Boy,* and *Pink Lady* in the original and was thrilled by the experience. When she came back, however, she had one of her unique criticisms.

"They're hung wrong," she objected. "They're side-by-side, but they are looking away from each other. Those museum people should hang them so they can see each other." It wasn't a joke; she was perfectly serious.

All in all, she was a delightful guest, very independent in spite of her age and total deafness. She occasionally joked about the troubles her heirs would have in dealing with the Big House, but she never let on that I was one of the people she was talking about.

I'm glad she came west those three years. Aside from the fact that she escaped the shut-in world of an East Coast winter the country, I came to know, to love, and to respect her as I could not have otherwise. I had loved her since I was a child, of course, but knowing her as a adult was different. It brought something new to the relationship, and we could relate in a way we had not before, as adults.

From explicit notes that I found in the apartment that summer, but shared with no one, I discovered that she lived for almost thirty years in fear of the cancer from which Cousin Catherine had died. She was ignorant of medicine, but had, for years, kept, careful clinical records on her physical condition. It must have been an appalling burden for her to carry alone.

I have always wondered about her passing. My lover and I were just considering a fourth trip for her when she died.

At the age of eighty-seven, she died as she probably would have wished, in her sleep. One day, she was her usual active self. She went to bed that night and did not get up the next morning. It was undoubtedly the best possible way for her to go. The next day, her tenants missed her and, upon investigation, found that she had slept away her life in the night.

I wonder if she knew at the last minute or just slipped away in her sleep? I can only hope that she knew no fear before she crossed that last great divide. The neighbors who found her said that she looked peaceful.

When she died, she left a massive set of questions in my mind. Neither her varied and productive past life of Open Country nor her intelligence and lively interest in Los Angeles bore any relationship to the incredibly useless hoarding of the valuable and the valueless that I found at Open Country. What had happened to the woman that caused her to turn in upon herself, to cling to the old place and its contents, when she could have made life so much more pleasant for herself by selling and moving to a smaller place?

What hold did Open Country and its contents have on her? Why, especially during her years of acute discomfort after the Antonis left, did she cling to possessions while living in penury? Why had she risked destruction of the things she loved (for it was a miracle that none of the roof leaks had ruined anything important or truly valuable) rather than see them cared for by someone else? Why, after sixty years of productive living was she willing to commit herself to a life of penury and social sterility?

Had her deafness played a part in this second great crisis of her life? Even though she read lips with great facility, her deafness must have set her apart from the family life around her. When she visited me in Los Angeles, I learned that when people were not speaking directly with her and were in general conversation she seemed to retreat into herself, sometime humming tunelessly until the conversation came her way again.

Given this, had she been in essence living alone for many years before her brother and sister died, left out of much of the life that flowed around her in Open Country? When the appalling shock of the loss of the family fortune struck her, did she feel deceived by those whom she had trusted? And, did she then decide to take no one's counsel in future but her own? Or was love of possessions a family trait too deeply ingrained for her to root it out when she was faced with the need to sell?

How could a woman be happy to follow such an empty path and then awaken to full interest and curiosity when she was presented with the new and different things she saw on the West Coast? How could she be content thereafter to return to her old life? Or was it that she took delight in little things like the bird feeder outside her living room window in the garage apartment, the growth of the plants she nurtured in the greenhouse, the flow and change of seasons, the production of fruits and vegetables she engaged in until the end? I will always wonder, but I can never know.

My reverie was abruptly shattered by a jerk as the train came to a stop in Grand Central Station, and I prepared to meet Mr. Quinn. His office was in the Empire State Building, just a few blocks away, and the rain had apparently stopped so I decided to walk there rather then wait for a bus.

His office was on about the seventieth floor. When I got there, I found that the clouds that, down below, had seemed to threaten rain, were actually swirling around the office windows. Mr. Quinn greeted me kindly, waved me to a chair that commanded the view, and gazed at me reflectively. He was a short man, in his sixties, partially bald, with twinkling eyes. He wore pince-nez glasses without rims or ear-pieces, a type much favored by older men and women in generations past.

His office was a model of precision. Various case files were stacked on his desk, their edges lined up neatly; his pipe rack was carefully centered with his humidor and a large ashtray placed on either side to balance each other. There was a bookcase full of books behind him, and the other furnishings included his own chair, comfortable chairs for his clients, and various diplomas and other official and quasi-official documents framed in dark wood and hanging on the walls.

Sitting across from him in one of his chairs, I wondered how often Cousin Margaret had sat in that same chair, and how she had come to retain him as her lawyer. Mr. Quinn filled and lighted his pipe and then gazed at me reflectively through his pince-nez, apparently preparing to deliver one of those philosophic lectures that elderly lawyers are often fond of giving. I was not disappointed. After engaging in preliminary pleasantries about my trip, he leaned back in his chair.

"Miss Leverich was a difficult client," he said, "especially when I tried to tell her something that she did not want to understand. That deafness of hers was a remarkably effective weapon when she chose to use it. If we got into an argument, and we did many times, she would just turn her head away from me, or shut her eyes, so she couldn't see my lips."

"I remember well." I smiled to myself. "She used that method for years. Once, when she and my mother got into an argument, Cousin Margaret turned her head away and Mother just walked out of the room before she had a chance to look back."

Mr. Quinn chuckled quietly and went on. "Many times I wished I could do that same thing. I inherited her, you know (I hadn't), from another lawyer. Miss Leverich didn't trust men, and, after her sister died, she retained a woman lawyer, Ethel Lawrence. Miss Lawrence was an associate with this firm for twenty years before she died. After she died, Miss Leverich came to me."

Small wonder, I thought, remembering what her dominating brother Henry had done to her. I began to like Mr. Quinn. His pipe had gone out, and he relit it. When he continued to speak, he was surrounded by a cloud of tobacco smoke rather like the swirling rain clouds outside.

Mr. Quinn frowned. "A remarkable woman, your cousin. Strong-willed and in many ways tragic. Your cousin was both blessed and cursed by money. Few people have lived so well, and fewer still have sacrificed so much in personal comfort and happiness to leave a legacy behind them for others to enjoy." I was to grow more horrified by this statement as the summer went on.

"When I took over her affairs after Miss Lawrence died, she was still living in the servants' wing of the Big House. Her only heat in the wintertime came from that old stove in the laundry room and the little radiator in the room above. Why she didn't freeze to death, I don't know.

"I was approached by a neighbor one winter day when I went up to see her. 'I came over the other evening to pay the rent,' he said, 'And I heard Miss Margaret crying in the kitchen. I walked in and found her down on her hands and knees on the cold, dirty kitchen floor trying to saw a soup bone in half with an old, rusty saw. The butcher had not cut her soup bone in half to fit her pot as he said he would, and the kitchen was full of smoke because the stove wouldn't draw properly. She was sawing away like mad and crying in pure frustration. I have never felt so sorry for anyone in my life.

"Other tenants told me of finding her hovering over the just-lit laundry stove on winter mornings, warming her hands while her teeth chattered in the winter cold. The kitchen episode was the final straw for me, and I resolved to get her out of the Big House and into that little apartment over the garage."

With some discomfort, I remembered that she had been maintaining her greenhouse next to the garage at a temperature of seventy degrees or so year-round during that entire period so that she could maintain her tropical plants.

I also remembered hearing through the family grapevine about her initial resistance and finally about the move from the house and I wondered what had happened. It was probably the only time that she was bulldozed into doing something she really did not want to do. And, as I was to learn, it took two people, her lawyer and a cooperative gardener, to do that.

Mr. Quinn continued.

"It was a major achievement to get her out of the house, to get her to make the garage apartment livable, and to give herself some comfort. I don't know if I could have done it if a water pipe leading to the big house had not burst. When her old gardener," Mr. Quinn stopped for a moment, "What's his name …?"

For a moment, he shuffled the papers on his desk looking for Cousin Margaret's file. "Ah, here it is. Matt. Matt Silichner. When Matt told her it could not be repaired, she finally agreed to move." Mr. Quinn's eyes twinkled. I wondered what he had said to Matt before the verdict on the pipe was rendered to my cousin.

The twinkle died from Mr. Quinn's eyes, and he looked sad. Turning away from me to gaze at the shifting clouds outside for a moment, he went on.

"Mr. Hunter, I have the deepest sympathy for those who have lost their wealth and assured position in society. 'Clipping coupons' is not an occupation, it is a way of life. The so-called idle rich are not idle at all. They use their wealth to advantage, improving themselves and the world around them. The only difference between them and the rest of us is that they can choose what they want to do, and the rest of us have to work for a living. The wealthy find ways to make themselves useful to society and they make a place for themselves in the world. The term 'idle rich' is a cruel misnomer, an expression dreamed up by rabble-rousers."

Quite right, I thought to myself, remembering the work that Cousin Margaret and Cousin Catherine had done out of the sense of civic duty that was expected of people in their position.

Mr. Quinn turned back to me and frowned.

"They get in trouble when they lose their money. Because they are thrust into a world they do not understand." He raised his eyebrows, placing the clasp of his pince-nez in some jeopardy. "How can they? Late in life, they have to fend for themselves in a way they had never known before. When their wealth is gone, they are surrounded by problems they are not equipped to deal with. I call them the new poor."

Thinking of my cousin in the ice-cold kitchen, I suddenly thought back to my own years in the army, remembering how the people in war-torn France had crowded around the trash cans outside our mess tents in winter, taking directly from our mess tins the meats and vegetables we did not wish to finish. Some of them had been my cousin's age, and I felt a reflection of the guilt and sorrow that had plagued me then.

"Miss Leverich was one of these. Because she was deaf, she had two strikes against her. Her brother and sister had always shielded her, and before them, her mother. When the storm struck, she was completely unprepared. Nothing she knew was important anymore."

How absurd, I thought, and yet he was right. Cousin Margaret had clung fiercely to Open Country, she had kept gardeners on until the war came, and she had continued to pay house servants until after the war. After the Antonis left because she could no longer afford their wages, she continued to cook and heat the servants' wing, filling the kitchen and laundry stoves with wood cut by Matt in his spare time. She wouldn't give up. My mother used to criticize her, saying she wanted to live the life of a country gentlewoman when she couldn't support it. And yet, what else was there for her? Wasn't it all she knew?

I remembered going to the house one time after the Antonis had left and Cousin Margaret had begun to live in the servants' wing because she could no longer heat or otherwise maintain the Big House. It must have been one of my last visits there before the rift which separated us for some fifteen years.

She took my parents out to the garden to gather the basket of vegetables that Open Country always provided for guests while I stayed in the Big House. Wandering through the halls, I finally came to Cousin Margaret's former bedroom. To my surprise, I found that the bed was neatly made and turned down as if for use, a pair of embroidered red silk slippers laid out neatly beside the bed. Cousin Margaret might be living in the servants' wing, but she would not let the casual visitor know.

Mr. Quinn swung around and reached behind him for a worn book on a bookshelf. "Henry Seidel Canby," he said. *"Home in the Nineties."* He riffled through the pages looking for the passage he wanted and began again, "The slow crushing of a family by its home ... yet still the shrinking remnant of the family held on from use and wont, or deep affection, until, in a final scene with depleted capital or broken health, the hollow shell of the home collapsed on a ruined estate and fiercely quarreling heirs."

A bitter chill went down my spine at that description and by the way it fitted my cousin's final years. The decline had begun with the Crash of 1929. In the years that followed, her brother, Cousin Henry, had dissipated his sisters' money through ill-advised investment and downright theft, paving the way for my cousin's final penury.

The telephone rang. Mr. Quinn answered it and then, like a man who has just remembered an appointment, stood up. My interview with him was at an end.

"I'm grateful," he said, "for Miss Leverich's winter visits to you on the West Coast. They gave her an enormous lift each year, one that she badly needed. Thank you for coming to see me. I have wanted to meet you for several years, but it would not have been appropriate until now."

On my side, I was grateful as well. Mr. Quinn was plainly one of those old-fashioned lawyers who had their clients' interests at heart and whose cash clock was not always running when talking to one of them. Still, I left in something of a daze. I had not thought of Cousin Margaret in the terms he described. I had, of course, known that she had lived in reduced circumstances, but the full cruelty of those circumstances had never hit me as did the force of Mr. Quinn's words.

As the elevator plunged down toward the street level, I began to think again. My childhood playmate was no more; the inquisitive and childlike adult I had known on the West Coast was also gone. All that was left was the shell of the house I had known from my childhood and young adulthood. That and fond memories of my little cousin.

On the way back on the train, my thoughts turned again to Open Country. My Cousin Lloyd's letters had painted a grim picture of its remains, something that did not entirely surprise me given what I had seen there during my visit there after my mother died.

My thoughts next turned to my planned private visit to the house the next day. What, I wondered would I find there? What was left of the gracious home I had once known? To what extent would Open Country still bear the imprimatur of my little cousin? More to the point, how painful was I going to find it to dismantle a home that I had known and loved as a child?

Chapter 3

Patton Crosses Rhine in a Daring Drive

The day after my visit to Mr. Quinn dawned as lowering and cheerless as the day before, and I borrowed Tom and Dorli's car for my solo visit to Open Country. The rain that had threatened when I left Wilton began to pepper my windshield as I turned into the driveway. My first view of the place was hardly reassuring. One of the stone posts guarding the driveway leaned drunkenly to one side, and the other was hidden by an overgrown privet hedge. Beyond the gate, I could see the row of maples that had always shaded the graceful curves of the gravel driveway leading to the house itself.

In my youth, they had shadowed the driveway pleasantly. Noble, elegant, well-trimmed maples with trunks at least four feet in diameter. In summer, they had provided pleasant shade after the harsh bright sun of the highway outside. In winter, their bare branches had arched over cars, letting the winter sun through and providing a gesture of welcome.

Now they were unkempt giants, their branches sweeping the ground, their leaves blocking the light from the leaden sky overhead, their dead branches littering the ground. So great was the gloom that I almost reached forward to turn on the car's headlights. In place of the pleasant welcome of former years, there was almost an atmosphere of menace as in a Charles Addams scene. Nature had closed in on the Open Country of my childhood and created in me an ominous feeling.

I picked my way up the driveway, with broken branches scrunching under the tires of my car and the wheels skidding occasionally on ruts worn by years of rain on the once-smooth gravel. As I rounded the final curve, the house itself appeared through the trees, a gray, gaunt ruin. The white paint had completely peeled from the shingles and trim and one shutter hung by a rusty hinge while others lay disconsolately on the porch roof. The graceful columns that had once supported the porch had been replaced here and there with bare, unpainted two-by-fours. Rotten roof members stuck out over these temporary supports like the broken teeth of an old comb. The outside porch light had lost both its globe and bulb, and the porch ceiling boards sagged in spots, showing black rot above. Through the windows in the dining room, I could see the roller blinds, water-stained and rotten, hanging in strips.

I felt almost fearful as I approached that great, gaunt ruin and became aware that I felt somewhat hesitant about entering the house itself. I told myself that that was foolish, and, leaving the car where we used to park, I walked over to the front steps. The once-spotless white Vermont marble bottom step was in place, though covered with mud, but the three wooden steps above it were loose and rotten. I walked gingerly up their edge and along the porch.

To my surprise, I found that the lawn in front of the house was neatly cut as in years past, and the porch still commanded the view of distant hills that gave the estate its name. If I had only looked across the lawn at the still well-dressed fieldstone wall and the view beyond, I could have been stepping back into the past.

In any case, I wondered why the lawn was so neat when all else was in ruin. Had my cousin … but at the age of eighty-seven that was unlikely. More probably it was one of the old retainers who came back to give what help they could to "Miss Margaret." A gesture harking back to the Sunset Age of her youth.

I walked along the porch, skirting little pools of water from the leaking roof. As I did so, the sound of my own footsteps echoing from the porch roof overhead carried me back once again to my childhood. How many times had I heard that echo coupled with Cousin Margaret's energetic steps, or footfalls that foretold the approach of Mrs. Antoni with the tea tray and her currant butter cake? The "Ghost of Summers Past" walked with me as I listened to the rain sprinkling what was left of the porch roof.

Slipping back into that past, I walked around the corner to the place where my cousin, my parents, and I used to sit and have tea overlooking Cousin Margaret's flower garden. My reminiscences were abruptly shattered by the reality before my eyes. The flower garden, once Cousin Margaret's pride, was gone. Disappeared. Where there had once been phlox, peonies, and roses in stately rows there was now only a tangle of plants and bushes.

Bayberry, boxwood, and the wisteria that had been brought from Newtown forty or more years before had taken over and made green jungle of a space once orderly and bright with flowers. To complete the scene, the porch floor where I stood had given way completely and sagged to within inches of the damp earth underneath. The porch ceiling sagged above, as if in company with the floor.

As can sometimes happen, odors carried me back to the past. First was the odor of boxwood, a dry, acrid-smelling bush used as borders in formal gardens in England and in this country. I remembered the scent both from Open Country and from the restored gardens of Williamsburg, where they are trimmed into the fanciful shapes popular in the eighteenth century. Cousin Margaret's, however, had been less than knee-high and neatly squared to frame the flower beds. These borders were now rough hedges six feet in height, and they dominated the ruins of the garden.

Added to the boxwood was the sweet, early summer smell of blooming syringa. We had had similar bushes at Lacey Green, and I had other associations with the smell as well. There was a big syringa bush outside the French doors to the living room, and its smell carried me back to the War. This area had been redolent with its odor in 1943, when I visited my cousin for the last time before going into the army; a few days later at Camp Upton, to my surprise, I had smelled it again. There was a row of syringa bushes outside our barracks, and I assuaged my initial homesickness with their fragrance. Now, of all the blooming flowers in the garden that I remembered, only the big syringa bush remained as it had been, reminding me poignantly of that bygone era.

Leaving the garden, I passed through the green gate that had always seemed so mysterious to me when I was a child because I had never seen what was behind it. No one ever seemed to use the gate, and I had been vaguely fearful of it, as if some unknown monster might escape if I opened it.

Aside from my own car, there was no sign that anyone was around, and I felt very isolated. After months of waiting, after flying three thousand miles, I was back on territory at once familiar and strange. And there was no one here to greet me. I felt lonely, very lonely.

My outside tour complete, my mind turned to the house and its contents—and to my last visit several years earlier, when my cousin had refused to let me enter the house. This time, my curiosity would be satisfied. I approached the servants' wing, looking for a way to get in.

A careful inspection of the south-facing windows showed that the glazier's putty had dried, a tribute to many years of neglect. Breaking into the house seemed no crime, and I did not want to wait for my cousins and their keys. My first visit to the empty rooms must be mine and mine alone so that I could come to terms with Open Country without being distracted by other people. Carefully removing some of the glazier's points, I gingerly took out a pane of glass close to a window latch. Reaching in, I turned the latch, raised the windows, and climbed into the servants' dining room.

I was struck first by the smell, a mustiness composed of dampness, dust, dry rot, and the leavings of mice that I associated with well-kept earthen cellars in the days of coal-fired furnaces and water heaters. I wrinkled my nose at once, for it was the sad smell of decay, of a house emptied of people, emptied of love and hate and all the things that make up life. It was the smell of dying and of death.

That musty odor, which also managed to include the yeasty smell of grapes, suggesting that wine had been made at Open Country in times past, haunted us all summer. It never left the house, no matter how many windows we opened, no matter how bright the sun outside.

Walking into the kitchen, I found ruin and disorder where I had previously known order, warmth, and the rich smells of good food. The kitchen was now cold, disordered, and empty. The ceiling was a dirty yellow, and the paint was peeled and scabrous, hanging in curls from the ceiling where it had not fallen away completely. The old wood stove had never been replaced with a modern range, and in my youth it had always been black-leaded till it gleamed, its nickel oven handles as silvery as when it first left the factory.

Now, its top warped by the fires of former years, it sat silently in rusty malevolence, its surface covered with curlicues of paint peeled from the ceiling. The octagonal Seth Thomas Regulator clock, whose measured beat used to mark time for us all, was silent. Because I could not stand that silence and wanted to bring a little life to the room, I wound the clock and set the pendulum to swinging. Its measured, off-center beat brought back a shadow of life and former times to the kitchen, and I welcomed it in the desolation that surrounded me.

The ticking of the clock provided for me a connection between the remembered past and the present. Like the clock, the home that was Open Country had run down and come to a stop sometime in the fifties, when a broken water pump had forced Cousin Margaret's removal to the former chauffeur's quarters.

So undisturbed was this rest that, when Mrs. Antoni came over and was offered something "to remember Miss Margaret by," she made a beeline for the kitchen and found her favorite baking tin, the only thing she wanted, in its customary place, exactly where she had left it eighteen years before. The house had remained in suspended animation until Cousin Margaret went to bed one night and failed to get up again the next morning.

The child in me was immeasurably saddened by the ruin before my eyes and the odors that now filled my nostrils. My adult self was more ready to accept the sadness, the sense of loss of childhood pleasure in the house—though I still found it difficult to bear.

Across the kitchen, a cabinet stood open. Curious, I looked in. Dirt, a few empty Baker's Chocolate tins of a prewar vintage, rusty pudding molds, and a cookie cutter. In a corner stood the electric mixer, once the pride of the kitchen, its bright paint contrasting with the desolation surrounding it. Looking at it, I remembered the summer it was first introduced and the rash of soufflés and whipped desserts that followed its arrival, the kitchen staff no longer having to beat by hand.

I pulled open one of the drawers. It was full to the brim with empty matchboxes. Two other drawers contained more of them. Why? In other drawers I found a stack of flattened waxed cardboard containers that had once contained butter. At first I was puzzled, and then I remembered that Cousin Margaret had used them to freeze her summer produce. The "Save That String" of her visits to the West Coast had been carried to extremes.

Passing through the butler's pantry, I entered the dining room. The tattered shades were drawn, the room gloomy and dark. The Duncan Phyfe dining table and chairs had disappeared, along with the portrait of Grandpa Leverich that used to preside over our meals. I shuddered briefly as I recalled sitting in those chairs during the many dinners I had enjoyed in that room, especially the wafer-thin fried eggplant slices that were another of Mrs. Antoni's specialties

Gone too was the still-life of dead ducks that used to fascinate me when I was a child. Somehow, they had always been more interesting to me than the stern features of Cousin Margaret's progenitor. The deer's skull and antlers, however, still hung in their place in a dark corner.

I flipped the light switch. Nothing happened. I raised the shades, tearing one, but little light came from outside and even less was reflected from the stained wallpaper. I looked around again. Across the room, I saw the dark shape of the giant mahogany sideboard that had been there since before I was born. Curious, I snapped on my flashlight and opened one of the doors. Like a single ray of sunshine seen through a chink in a curtained room, a vase of iridescent Tiffany Favrile glass gleamed back at me from the darkness. I shook my head in disbelief and, unbelieving, I took its green and gold sparkle in my hands.

A vase of Tiffany glass in the *art nouveau* style that replaced Victorian pomposity at the turn of the century. The proof of authorship, "LCT-Favrile-Y4568," was inscribed on the bottom. Louis Comfort Tiffany, an authorship long predating the current "Tiffany and Company."

Even more of a surprise, the paper label was still attached to the bottom, indicating that, in the probably sixty years or so that had passed since its purchase, it had never been washed. How long had it sat in the sideboard and why was it never used? Some ill-chosen Christmas or birthday present given before 1910 and put away because the recipient did not like it?

And why had it not been sold among other things in the past thirty years? Or was it possible that the house contained more than the trash that I had assumed? When first told of the legacy by Mr. Quinn, I thought that our real task was to clear out and dispose of trash so that our tiny cousin would not be disgraced. Had her parting gift to us been something different? Was the vase in my hands a harbinger of things to come? Might my share of the inheritance consist of more than empty match boxes and corroded cookie cutters? Thoughtfully, I replaced the green and gold glitter in the darkness from which it had come.

As I did so, I noticed half-a-dozen rather nice cut crystal sherry glasses shoved into the shadows in the back. Since I never remembered sherry being served at Open Country, even after the repeal of Prohibition, I wondered how long they had been there.

Closing the sideboard door, I walked into the main entrance hall that was the central feature of the house. Even in the half-light of that rainy day, it remained as impressive as I remembered it, the ceiling soaring two-and-a-half stories above the floor. That entrance hall formed the base of a deep *U*. Opposite a *V*-shaped staircase facing the front door, there was a set of clerestory windows lighting a gallery running around the other three sides. This gallery led to three bedrooms and to the suite of rooms leading to Cousin Margaret's room at the far end of the wing. Beneath this suite of rooms was the hallway leading to the big sunken living room.

The clerestory windows were shaded by the trees outside and let in little light. Standing in that gloomy hall, I felt the need to bring in some light and air. I opened the wide Dutch front door that led out to the lawn and the hills beyond and looked outside. It was raining dismally now, and the black clouds and towering maples conspired to keep out much of the daylight. Against the wall outside, I saw the columns that used to support the porch, rotted beyond repair but stacked neatly against the house. The scent of wet leaves was refreshing after the mustiness of the house, and I stood there for a few moments, looking over the view of lawn and hills beyond before turning back inside.

In my childhood, the hall had been impressive, with a giant fieldstone fireplace surrounded by chairs and an enormous Persian rug, and a great bronze, turn-of-the-century globed chandelier dominating the whole. I looked into the ground-floor bedroom where the sisters and their brother had had their famous fight and where both Cousin Henry and Cousin Catherine had later died. There was no furniture in the room, and the floor was covered with plaster because the ceiling had fallen in. The floor boards were buckled with dampness.

After a few minutes, I walked over to a corner of the hall and turned the light switch. The globes of the chandelier leapt to light, revealing harsh cracks and bulges in the walls that had not been apparent before. The chandelier was green with verdigris, and the stairs were covered with plaster fallen from the wall and from the ceiling above. On the top of a sideboard set against the wall was a vase of bayberry seeds routinely picked during the fall and kept there during the winter as a promise of summer.

I looked into the sideboard, finding bottles and jars, each with a label and a date: "Currant Jelly (1944)" (made with scarce wartime sugar!), "Mrs. A's Tomato Pickle (1944)," "Raspberry Vinegar (1955)," "Orange Marmalade (1956)."

There was even a comb of the rich, dark buckwheat honey I used to spread on Mrs. Antoni's home-baked bread when I was small. I picked one of the compartments open with my fingernail and tested the contents. It was still good, a satisfying mixture of rich honey and beeswax. Saddened, I put it down. Like the clock in the kitchen, Open Country's productivity had stopped, leaving only the culinary ghosts of the past.

Continuing on my way, I turned toward the old living room. Newspapers filled the floor of the hall leading to the flower room, sharing it with wicker baskets of neatly washed and stacked tin cans. I glanced at a paper at random and found it to be the *New York Times*, dated March 24, 1945, that featured the headline "Patton Crosses Rhine in a Daring Drive."

I picked it up and saw a second headline, "New Rhine Bridgehead Won/Without the Loss of a Single Man." The accompanying photograph showed the pontoon bridge on which I, myself, had crossed the Rhine that same day. It seemed strange to be reading about a wartime exploit of mine then more than twenty years in the past.

I was tempted to read the story to find out whether the story included Patton's boast that he had pissed in the river on his way across. I immediately realized, however, that I would never see the rest of the house if I got involved in newspaper articles dating from World War II, and I put it down with some regret.

Evidently, both the papers and the cans had been saved for World War II salvage drives and never picked up. Amid the clutter on the floor sat the marble mantel clock from the living room, its ponderous elegance looking more than a little out of place.

I was startled by a rattling sound as I went down the steps to the living room. It was a peculiarity of the house when I was a child, that greeting. Whenever anyone passed through the hall leading to the living room, the plates on the Franklin stove nearby rattled. No one could ever figure out why, so visitors to the living room were announced that way for more than forty years.

Looking into the flower room, once Cousin Margaret's province, I found a surprise. It was an island of neatness. The sink was clean and the vases were arranged in neat rows as if waiting for her to come in from the garden, a basket of flowers over her arm. She must have taken care that the room remain neat and tidy, for the place was spotless. Even the floor was clean. I sighed at the sight and moved on.

At the top of the stairs leading to the sunken living room, I paused, peering down through the gloom. The wisteria vine that used to shade the French doors leading to the flower garden had run amok and had almost covered the doors completely. Great, heavy trunks hung in festoons between the porch supports. The vine had twisted and broken the fragile woodwork lattice and wound around the uprights so that it seemed a tossup whether the wisteria was supporting the porch or seeking to tear it down from the house. The vines created a malevolent atmosphere that made me shudder as I walked down the steps.

Across the room, the fireplace stood filled with pails set to catch rainwater, and I then saw why the living room clock was no longer in its usual place. Dampness had warped the mantelpiece into a shallow bow, and the nearby plaster had disintegrated and fallen in neat piles against the baseboard as if swept there. The figured wallpaper hung before the bare lathes like a curtain, its pattern faded but undisturbed. I walked over and touched a piece. It was damp and soft like old felt, and it came away in my hand gently and without a sound. I dropped it onto the pile of plaster that it had once covered.

The sofa where Cousin Catherine used to sit was gone, but its twin remained, the red silk rotted but unfaded, the color probably preserved inadvertently by the wisteria that covered the windows. The fine eighteenth-century corner chair my father used to sit in was there, but out of place. Chairs stood at odd angles around the room like people frozen in mid-gesture at a cocktail party, and a Chinese lamp stood on a trestle table, socket empty, the shade torn and askew. There were two bright notes in the room: a pair of clear blue Venetian glass vases on top of a bookcase near one of the French doors.

Bemused by the clutter and wandering through the shadows, I opened a drawer here, a cabinet there. There was a complete set of the New York Social Register 1902–1936, the last being the year of my Cousin Catherine's death, and a drawerful of carefully wrapped jigsaw puzzles. One of them bore the notation, in Cousin Margaret's hand, "97 pieces, 3 missing." Mesmerized, I was almost tempted to recount. I opened another package and found a pair of gold-rimmed spectacles with a notation in Cousin Margaret's hand, "MDL does not know to whom these belonged."

I found bronze and marble Italian souvenirs from the turn of the century or before in a drawer, as well as two dozen silver lamé paper cigarette holders dating from the twenties. They had probably belonged to my Cousin Henry's wife, Jessie.

A Swiss music box caught my eye. I turned it over and looked at its bottom. I read *Valse de la Grande Duchesse; La Vie Parisienne No. 6* in faded ink. I wound it up and set it back in its place. The last sound I heard as I left the room was its plaintive little tune. I later wondered who finally bought it.

By that time, I was feeling confused. Very much so. I needed some respite from the sheer volume of material that I had found. Returning to the main hall, I found a little side chair set against a wall. I took this outside and sat looking at the neatly cut lawn and thinking about other times when I had enjoyed the view of distant hills from that vantage point. Presently, my sense of normalcy returned, and I decided to look upstairs.

Returning to the main hall, I climbed the stairs to the second floor and looked into some of the bedrooms that opened onto the hall gallery. The first I entered was so full of boxes and barrels that I could barely get in. I picked an open barrel at random and looked into it. I found that it was full of small packages wrapped in tissue paper. Opening one, I found that it contained an oriental demitasse cup so delicate that an eggshell would seem coarse by comparison. A second contained a Chinese export coffee cup that matched a pair that I had at home.

Chinese export porcelain was brought around Cape Horn in sailing vessels, and that cup belonged to a set that dated to about 1760. That Cousin Margaret had one, and probably more, that matched mine was not surprising since we had ancestors in common. Carefully, I rewrapped the two cups and put them back where I had found them. Bemused by the immensity around me, I shook my head, set them aside and moved on to the next room

The adjacent bathroom contained three enormous caribou heads that I did not remember seeing before, though they may have been a result of some Western hunting expedition of Cousin Henry's. They lived there all summer because we did not know where else to put them. Evidently Cousin Margaret hadn't either, and they delighted visitors, child and adult alike, all summer.

Continuing on around the balcony, I found the next room all but destroyed by rain coming down from the attic above, accounting for the water damage in the ground-floor bedroom below. The ceiling and much of the wall plaster had given way. The room was chill, damp, and empty except for a French wardrobe in the style of Louis Phillipe. I opened it and found it empty. Poking into dresser drawers in another bedroom, I found more packages wrapped in paper, while adjacent closets disclosed rows of dresses and cardboard containers containing still more packages.

Walking down the hall toward the Green Room, where I had slept as a child, and Cousin Margaret's bedroom beyond, I came to the bathroom that stood out over the porch below. The floor was askew, and the whole room creaked slightly as I walked in. Remembering the collapsed porch below and fearful that it would collapse under my weight, I hastily retreated to the safety of the hall.

Passing through the sewing room and other bedrooms, I noted a fine satinwood Federal bureau, a Chippendale double chest of drawers and an Italian inlaid chest of drawers. As elsewhere, these pieces of furniture were full of little packages wrapped in paper. In the sewing room, I also found a row of foot-treadle sewing machines that predated electric Singers and would have been used for dressmaking in years past.

When I came to the Green Room (so-called because of its wall coloring), the powerful odor of urine struck my nostrils. I opened a bureau drawer and found it full of mouse fuzz, wet from recent occupancy. Hastily I threw the contents out of a window and set the drawer aside to air.

Opening the closets and bureau drawers, I found stacks of paintings, prints in good gilt frames, family papers, fans, and a great many dresses of that indeterminate style once favored by ladies of the Helen Hokinson cartoons in the *New Yorker*. I also found one yellow satin number, clearly from the twenties, ornamented with gold lace, beadwork, and sequins. Since I could not imagine either

Cousin Margaret or her sister wearing it, it must have belonged to Cousin Jessie.

Cousin Margaret's former bedroom was tidy and still contained the fine sleigh bed she used to sleep in, neatly turned down, with the same pair of red-and-gold embroidered slippers still placed tidily by its side, where I had seen them more than twenty years before. Poking into her closets and bureau drawers, I found more of what I had found elsewhere: articles of clothing (some quite old), and packages wrapped in paper.

Looking through her closets brought to mind the trunks of ancestral dresses in the attic above. Pulling down the disappearing staircase from the hall ceiling outside her bedroom, I walked up and found about a dozen trunks in a neat row. I opened a few of them and raised the tissue paper covering the dresses. The silks and velvets were bone dry, their color undimmed, their texture unspoiled. Even the fragile magnificence of Grandma Schuchardt's wedding dress seemed untouched by time. At the far end of the attic, I could see daylight through cracks in the roof and realized that it lay above the ruined rooms below. Hastily, I opened the few trunks at that end of the attic and found them empty. Evidently, Cousin Margaret had taken the things out of that portion of the attic and stored them below in the bedroom wing.

I heaved a sigh of relief, for I had long hoped to see the dresses donated to some museum. I shut the trunks again and walked back down stairs. On the way, I noticed six wooden fireplace mantels yawning at me. I did not remember them, but they must have come from the Newtown House, whose remains were stacked at the back of the property. As I walked to the stairs, the glint of gilt caught my eye from deep under the eaves. Reaching down, I found a gilt and cloisonné card tray from the eighties partly hidden by wrappings in a wooden box.

I had one more place to reconnoiter—the cellar. Returning downstairs, I found two doors leading there. The first stood closed amid a pile of fallen plaster and was stuck tight with damp. The second was only slightly stuck and opened with a wooden grunt. To my surprise, the electricity below worked. In the dim 15-watt light, I saw a clutter of broken crocks and wine bottles, preserving jars, empty barrels, and a giant stack of cut firewood. In the corner, there was a litter of crates that seemed to contain marble. Like the mantels in the attic, these must have been brought up from Long Island with the Newtown House remnants that had been rotting on the property for years.

When I was through with the cellar and had wandered back outside, I found myself confused by the enormity of the job before us. I had counted a total of twenty-nine rooms, three attics, and a full cellar. There were closets in every room, chests of drawers, desks, wardrobes, and innumerable cardboard boxes and barrels, all full.

The house was like a recreation of the Collyer Brothers house in New York City, a story that had hit the newspapers when I was a copy boy at the *New York Daily Mirror* in the early 1950s. The Collyers had been wealthy recluses for years, until they both died; the stench of their rotting bodies had finally led the police to break into the house to locate the source. They discovered that the brothers had been pack rats for years. They had never thrown anything out, for years crawling through tunnels under stacks of old newspapers that made it difficult even to find the two dead men. Still, the parallel was there in that my little cousin had sought to preserve and label everything in the house … for whom?

How were we to deal with it all? So much of it seemed to be trash interspersed with things of value. In one drawer, for example, I found a box of squares ready to be made into an afghan and a number of incomplete petit-point cushion covers. Elsewhere, there was that pair of spectacles with the notation, "MDL does not know to whom these belonged" as well as little boxes containing women's fans. This went on for room upon room until I was ready to cry with fatigue at the thought of the work ahead.

With every room full, how would we ever be able to sort things out without becoming engulfed? Packed, a trunk or a closet occupies very little space. Unpacked, it could fill a room. How would we manage to unpack twenty-nine rooms, when even just one of them contained three closets, a wardrobe, a filing cabinet, a chest of drawers, and two built-in chests of drawers, all of them full?

Throughout my childhood, my parents had shaken their heads over the Leverich habit of accumulating. For all their wealth, they never seemed to have bought wastebaskets or learned to use them. Anything that had belonged to any member of the family, especially if deceased, assumed the sacred status of a Family Possession and could not be thrown away. What a normal household would have thrown away years or even decades before had been preserved.

Nor could we assume that it was all junk. The Tiffany vase, the Chinese export porcelain showed that they had squirreled away the valuable with the valueless. Every box, every little package wrapped with string would have to be unpacked, and that carefully.

This was the first time I had regarded my cousins' pack rat habits as anything but a family eccentricity. Now the problem had descended on me like a thundercloud and enveloped me completely. The house was like some incredibly large nightmare, with its great numbers of gloomy rooms, their figured wallpaper hanging in strips, their closets full of clothing, their innumerable chests, barrels, and boxes.

It all seemed like a nightmare too big to be believed. The feeling of decay, the sterility, the monumental ruin of a once prosperous and productive family seemed to have seeped into my very soul in the half hour that my tour had taken. The clutter, the jumble, the huge combination of the useless and the useful, the valueless and the valuable left me weary. I was tired before the task of sifting had even begun. As I was to learn later in the summer, this sifting, massive task though it was, was perhaps the easiest part of the whole process.

Walking back up to the ground floor, I let myself out the laundry room window, shutting it carefully behind me. As I left, I wondered at the rather bland descriptions I had received by letter from Lloyd Robertson. Much of his correspondence had involved separating "chaff from chaff." Had my two cousins not gotten beyond the servants' wing? Had they any idea about the rich variety of Leverich belongings that I had encountered in my short survey of the house?

As I drove back to Wilton and the relative sanity of Tom and Dorli's house, my thoughts continued to wander through the house from room to room, trying to absorb the multiplicity and variety of things that I had seen and experienced in my short trip through the building. For all that, I planned to return the next day, hoping that my cousins would be present so that we could start working, I found I was not looking forward to the prospect.

CHAPTER 4

We Have Found about Eighty Dollars in Cash Hidden Away

After leaving Open Country, I returned to Tom and Dorli's house to spend the night, and it was like returning to a sane world. I tried to explain the enormity of the house and its contents to them, but I was unable to make them understand. Both of them were skeptical. It couldn't be as bad as all that, they insisted. I could hardly blame them. After all, I had exchanged letters with Lloyd for several months and it had not registered.

The next morning, I borrowed Tom and Dorli's car again and drove to Open Country. The sun was shining; as a result, I felt more cheerful, and I reveled in the lush green of the East Coast, so different from the arid Southern California that I had come from. Roses were blooming, meadows were carpeted with daisies, and dandelions made golden patches in the lawns of the houses I drove past. Open Country's driveway seemed more cheerful than it had the day before, though the house appeared just as grim and forbidding.

Once again, there was no one there when I arrived. Entering by the same window I had used the day before, I wandered back through the house in something of a daze. Today I was to meet my cousins, and I wasn't sure what to do while waiting for them.

Presently, my wanderings took me to Cousin Margaret's old bedroom, if only because it was in the best state of repair and seemed homey. I began to look through some of the bureau drawers and found a lace fan, which I took out. There was a label on it that read, "Carried by Catherine at her coming-out party in 1894." I wondered if Cousin Margaret's hearing had been good enough for her to waltz at her sister's debut. Waltz only, of course, and with a dance card containing the names of those with whom she had agreed to dance. The days of ragtime were ten years in the future then, and "cutting in" was not yet considered proper. My reverie was interrupted by a shout.

"Hullo! Anyone here?" The sound came from the great hall below. Returning to the hall gallery, I looked down and saw a short man with a mustache and glasses looking up at me. He wore gray flannel trousers, a lumberjack shirt, and a crushed army fatigue cap; in one hand, he carried a pair of work gloves and in the other, a broom. He had a pipe clamped in his teeth, and there was a smell of good English Latakia tobacco in the air, its pungency somewhat masking the musty odor in the hall. The questioning look on his face gave way to a shy smile as I came down the stairs.

I recognized my cousin Lloyd Robertson. As I came down the stairs, he shifted his gloves to his left hand and took his pipe out of his mouth. Holding out his right hand, he said, "Hullo, old man. Good to see you at last."

Lloyd seemed very little changed since I had last seen him—in the middle of the thirties. He had put on weight, but he retained the shy, good-natured dignity that had characterized him as a young man. In those days, he had affected British reserve in speech and manner, and his pipe was part of that affectation. Age had added wrinkles around his eyes, and they gave his eyes a twinkle they had not had when he was young. Perhaps, too, he had been depressed when I last saw him. With that mother of his, it would not have been surprising.

As a child, I had been an avid train fan, as had he. We had spent many hours together watching the switching engines and an occasional passenger or freight train in the Mott Haven yards of the New Haven Railroad. It was wonderful for a child to share interests with an "older man" (he had been in his late teens at the time), and I had grown very attached to him, in part because my father was not as willing to share my interests as he had been. Lloyd had built superb scale models of New Haven rolling stock, complete with tracks and overhead wires for his engine and would occasionally let me play with them, but only under his supervision.

After a gap of some thirty years, Lloyd was remarkably undemonstrative. To my California way of thinking, something more than a quiet hello and a handshake seemed called for. Even my reserved New England friend Tom had embraced me warmly, and I had gotten a good proper hug from Dorli. At the same time, his British reserve did not at all disguise the fact that he was glad to see me.

Having shaken my hand in a very formal manner, Lloyd moved back a step and said, "I saw the car outside the garage and wondered who was here. When did you arrive?"

"Three days ago. I was able to get away early. I'm staying with friends in Wilton. I went to see Mr. Quinn day before yesterday, and then decided to drive over yesterday to look the place over. I took quite a tour of the house. Pretty awful isn't it?"

Lloyd's brows contracted in a worried frown. "How did you get in? We always lock up most carefully when we go. Did we leave something open?"

"No. Everything was locked up, but I took out a pane of glass in the laundry room and opened a window latch."

Lloyd gazed me reflectively and shifted his feet slightly, "Most enterprising of you, old fellow. Most distressing that you could do it so easily. I guess the old house is not exactly burglar-proof. I imagine you looked over the house pretty thoroughly?"

"Top to bottom. I went everywhere, from the attic to the cellar. It's bigger than I thought. And it's awful. I can't even imagine where to begin."

Busy footsteps clattered in from the direction of the kitchen and Lloyd's wife, Louise, appeared. She bustled in wearing a sturdy smock over a cotton dress, a pair of glasses and a small magnifying glass attached to cords around her neck. Lloyd turned to look at her with a cheerful smile and more emotion than he had yet shown.

"Look, old girl. Russell, at long last."

Louise stopped in the door of the dining room and looked at me with a cheerful smile.

"Oh, Russell, we're so glad you are here at last. I hoped it was you when I saw the strange car parked outside. Sorry we weren't here when you got here, but it's such a long drive up from Long Island that we seldom get here before ten. Have you been over to Cousin Margaret's apartment yet?" Her words came out in a rush, almost as if she were out of breath. She sounded like an eager teenager, though there was no immaturity in her manner.

"No. Only the main house. I jimmied a window and got in without trouble, but Cousin Margaret's apartment was locked and I couldn't get to the second story. I was hoping you'd get here soon."

"Well, we are certainly glad you are here. I've just made some coffee over in Cousin Margaret's apartment. Why don't we go over now and have a cup together? Afterward, we can come back here and get to work."

That sounded like a good idea. Anything to avoid figuring out where Square One was. Before she turned to go, my curiosity got the better of me.

"I'd love some coffee. And, by the way, why the magnifying glass around your neck?"

"To look at hallmarks and makers' marks on china and silver.

It's so much fun finding things, and I like to know who made them. From the makers' marks and initials, I try and figure out which member of the family owned them." Her delivery was again breathless, and I had an immediate picture of an inquisitive puppy eagerly following a scent.

She turned to Lloyd. "Remember that silver teapot in her apartment? The one where the initials are almost worn away by polishing? Well, I forgot to tell you, but after you went to sleep last night, I looked over the makers' marks in my silver book, and ..." still talking, Louise preceded us through the kitchen, followed by Lloyd, who was hanging on her words.

We walked out the kitchen door and into the June sunlight. Lloyd and Louise preceded me, Louise still chattering happily about her discovery. The smell of honeysuckle was in the air and, away from the awful decay inside, the world seemed to have returned to a measure of normalcy. The magnificent maples around the house were in full leaf, and an enormous rhododendron bush fully two stories high bloomed against the icehouse. There were bright crimson roses blooming on the fence hiding the service yard and, as I turned to follow its unpainted, weathered pickets back to the equally weathered shingles on the house, I was filled with pity. Open Country resembled a once-beautiful woman, now wrinkled and sagging in her old age.

As we walked toward the garage, I noticed that the vast expanse of the vegetable garden was bare except for six new tomato plants. I stopped immediately, and Louise turned around and saw me looking at them.

"I couldn't resist planting them. Cousin Margaret so loved growing things, and I thought we'd enjoy their fruit later in the summer."

At the base of the stairs to Cousin Margaret's apartment, I was struck by the heavy, humid scent of the greenhouse. Looking in, I saw that it was full of a variety of tropical and semi-tropical plants; there was clivia, sweet olive brought from a family plantation in

Natchez that had been sold fifty years before, orchids, lemon and rose geraniums, and other plants I did not recognize. I also saw a small oleander bush that I remembered had been a prize of hers. It was about four feet tall, and I contrasted that with the oleanders that grow wild in California to a height of twelve feet or more. There too, were the "exotic" plants that my cousin had brought East as cuttings from the West Coast.

Seeing this display, I understood why Cousin Margaret had denied herself so many comforts to keep the greenhouse going winter and summer. In the old days, the gardens had been her province and responsibility, and both in this greenhouse and in her small vegetable garden, at least she could continue the productivity of former years cultivating exotic plants and starting flats in spring for her vegetable garden.

Up above the greenhouse, her apartment was cheerful and cozy. She had a collection of miniature toy birds mounted in a sunny kitchen window and a bird feeding station right outside the panes. I also saw a can of birdseed next to the window and, after I moved into her apartment later in the summer, I put out birdseed as long as it lasted. My customers were very tame, and I could imagine my bright-eyed cousin watching them and wishing that she could hear what they were saying to each other. After I had used up the birdseed in midsummer, I stopped feeding them, feeling that they should learn to forage elsewhere before the chill of winter came upon them.

In her little living room, I recognized the Tiffany lamps and Chinese ebony tables I remembered from evenings by the fire in the living room in the Big House, and there was a small sofa and comfortable chairs standing about. It was a very cozy room. Lloyd and I sat in companionable silence while Louise busied herself with the coffee, and I thought back to the days when I had first met Louise.

Lloyd's mother, Kitty, was very jealous and possessive of her children, Lloyd in particular. To the distress of much of the family, she engineered it so that he neither went to college to learn electrical engineering, for which he was well-suited by talent, nor obtained a job. My father was particularly distressed over this since he felt that Lloyd was wasting his life. Kitty had been left well-off by her husband and had inherited further money when her mother had died. There was no financial pressure on the family, and Kitty was able to dominate her son up to a point. Until Lloyd fell definitively in love.

At that time, I had frequented the house a great deal because of my shared interest with Lloyd and my interest at watching his model railroad grow in size and complexity. Sometime in the mid-thirties, my parents decided that the atmosphere was not right for a growing boy and put a stop to the friendship.

To be honest, I think that the real reason (that they were probably not aware of) was jealousy. I was very attached to both Lloyd and his mother, Kitty, (one of a surfeit of Catherines and Katherines in the family). Kitty herself had some childlike characteristics and was a motherly soul. She and I used to enjoy outings to the FAO Schwartz toy store to look at the toy trains there, and I rather imagine that this grated on my jealous mother.

The problem, as explained to me, had to do with a lover that Kitty had had for many years, and who frequented the house a great deal. It is possible that my parents were honestly concerned, though why they were distressed over it I don't know. Gene was a very likeable man, always very nice to me. As for his relationship with Kitty, in those innocent years, a well-bred child my age might know where babies came from but certainly had little idea of how the process started. In a way, sex was abhorrent to us. I recall, when I was about thirteen, talking about sex with some of my friends. One of us made some remark about our parents having sex, and the reaction of one of them was instantaneous:

"*My* parents would never do anything like *that!*"

Quite where he thought *he* came from, I do not know.

About the same time that I was forbidden the Robertson

household, Lloyd fell in love. He fell in love most inappropriately with a nurse. Evidently, they had been doing *"that,"* and Mary Louise, as she was then called, had become pregnant. As a result, they married secretly and needed a place to live temporarily.

At about the same time, my parents were making plans for us to drive to the West Coast over the summer and wished to have someone guard the place and take care of it over the summer while we were gone. They were especially concerned because, during the previous summer, a local family, who lived on a back road, had gone on a trip and found their house gone when they returned.

Apparently the thieves knew the family was away for the summer and not only took the furniture but dismantled the house itself and removed it. The neighbors did not complain to the police, they said afterward, because they simply thought that the Stevens were moving. No one appeared to be interested in hiding what was going on, so there was no local suspicion.

"Supply met demand," as a friend of my mother's used to say, and Lloyd and Louise had stayed at Lacey Green for the summer, mowing the lawn and taking care of my father's precious gardens. We had a marvelous summer touring the West, and they had an equally good time living in the country and away from Kitty Robertson.

I had not seen either of them after that summer until now. Tragically, the baby miscarried, Mary Louise taking care of the delivery herself because Lloyd was away with the car. I never knew how or whether Kitty had become reconciled to the marriage. I never even learned whether Lloyd got a job or not.

I imagine that our gift of a summer at Lacey Green must have made Kitty furious, because I never heard of or from her again. I did not even hear when she died. Sometime in the intervening years, Lloyd and Louise had had two children, whom I was to meet later in the summer. This was, then, the first time that I had seen either of them for at least twenty-five years. I was glad that contact was restored, for I had found them both likeable people.

While we were waiting, Lloyd got out his pipe tobacco and carefully filled his pipe while Louise kept up a running flow of chatter from the kitchen.

"You saw the big pile of trash in the servants' wing? Mr. Quinn wouldn't let us throw away a thing until you arrived. We sent a load of cardboard boxes to the dump, but that was all. There was one whole room full of them upstairs. Lloyd dragged them out, threw them off the balcony into the hall, and took them out to the driveway.

"Cousin Margaret's old gardener, Matt, took them away. It cost us about twenty dollars just to get rid of them. How are we ever to get rid of all the rest? It will cost a fortune."

Fire, I thought to myself, remembering the broad expanse of the vegetable garden where burning would be safe. Somehow the idea appealed to me. Dumps are such public and depressing places.

I had had a lot of experience with using fire this way. At Lacey Green, we had no real dump (and of course in those days no garbage trucks) and so had quite frequently burned trash of one sort or another as a way of getting rid of it. Sometimes, personal effects were disposed of this way, and they vanished utterly in the process.

Surrounded as I was by the decay of the productive life I had once loved, I preferred to commit the wretched remains to some private *Götterdämerung* than to expose them publicly. Fire purifies, destroys completely, and leaves anonymous and unidentifiable remains.

Louise kept up her flow of chatter from the kitchen. "We do whatever appeals to us. We haven't really organized anything. The place is so huge, we just start somewhere and keep working. As you know, we cleared out the servants' wing. When that was done, we just moved into the rest of the house and got lost.

"We clear things out, and Lloyd hauls the trash to the back room, but we don't seem to accomplish anything." Louise sounded despondent.

She came in from the kitchen bearing coffee and sweet rolls. Lloyd continued to puff on his pipe quietly as she continued:

"Mr. Quinn says we can't take anything away until the appraiser comes. But we can unpack things. The house was broken into last winter, you know, but nothing was taken. After that, he did let us take the Duncan Phyfe table and chairs, Grandpa Leverich's portrait, and some china and silver down to Katherine's house."

"Will Katherine be here today?" I asked, wondering about my other cousin.

"I think so. She knows you are coming and is looking forward to seeing you again."

The talk then turned to other matters, and my own thoughts went to Katherine, whom I had known when she was in her late teens and I was still a child. She was tall, much taller than either her mother or brother, and strikingly blonde. Looking back, it seems as if she might have stepped off the stage of *Gentlemen Prefer Blondes* before it became a musical.

She collected nicknames. Her first, "Duchess," she had earned because she was a sleepwalker. Kitty had woken up one night feeling uneasy (Katherine was sixteen at the time, and probably going on much older) and had gone to Katherine's room to find Katherine sitting on the window sill, her legs dangling above the street six stories below.

For once in her life, Kitty hadn't given way to the hysteria for which she was famous. Instead, she had asked quietly,

"What are you doing, dear?"

"I'm looking for the duchess's handkerchief," was the dignified reply.

"That's all right, dear. It's been found. Now come on back inside."

Her second nickname was "Peaches"; I do not know where she got it, unless it was her complexion. In the days before tanning became a national pastime, a "peaches and cream" complexion was much admired. Looking back now, I have the additional suspicion that it was not unconnected with her resemblance to the Lorelei of the aforementioned Broadway play.

Katherine had gotten married in the thirties to an Englishman while I was still allowed to visit the household. I remember seeing her, heavily pregnant, some months after they were married. She had emigrated with him to England shortly after, but the transplant did not take. English life did not agree with her, and she returned to the United States with her child. I had not seen her, however, since that first marriage (and there had been several later ones).

Katherine arrived shortly after we finished coffee, driving an ancient Peugeot. From the kitchen window in the apartment, I watched as she unfolded her tall frame from the little car and saw that she had put on weight over the years. In her youth, she had been thin and statuesque. No more. She had even grown a "Schuchardt." In my youth, the term was a polite family euphemism for the over-large buttocks that were characteristic of the Dutch New York family from which we were all descended.

Katherine's clothing was serviceable but showed that she wanted to look well-dressed despite the heavy work we would be doing. She wore an attractive skirt and blouse and an informal brimmed straw hat. Her makeup was carefully applied and her wavy hair caught back in a tightly coiled bun at the back of her head.

Katherine strode across the lawn with a purpose that was lacking in either Lloyd or Louise and mounted the stairs with energy. Lloyd tended to amble; Louise bustled, but neither moved with purpose. I sensed immediately that Katherine could be a formidable adversary if so moved.

"Well, Cousin, it's been a long time," was the cordial greeting that preceded her through the door. The sound of the greeting was friendly, but there was an implied reminder that I was a *younger* cousin and not quite on her level. It also said something about her relationship with Lloyd that did not entirely surprise me. Additionally, as she entered, I sensed that she was keenly sizing up the newly arrived member of the partnership. I felt very much that she was pleased to see me (for, after all, I had been a very pleasant little boy) but that I was very much under inspection.

The words came in a throaty purr strongly reminiscent of Tallulah Bankhead (and perhaps copied from her?). Whatever the genesis, there was more than a suggestion of what my mother used to call a "come-hither" voice; the delivery suggested that Katherine could, therefore, be also be formidable in bed.

"It has indeed," I agreed. "Lloyd and Louise have been telling me all about your work here."

Katherine stood in the center of the room, feet apart, staring at me through her big almond-shaped eyes. "Have you been in the Big House yet?" she asked.

"Climbed in through a laundry room window yesterday and again today before Lloyd and Louise arrived. We were just about to go over and get to work when you arrived."

"Would you like some coffee?" This from Louise, who had been quietly washing the coffee cups and now stood in the kitchen door, a dish towel with a Palm Springs label on it in her hands.

"No, thanks. Perhaps we'd better get over to the Big House," Katherine replied.

She had lost her New York accent and had developed the peculiar clenched teeth method of delivery that Mother used to call "Hudson River Bracketed." Most certainly, it was fashionable Westchester County or Tuxedo Park. Conscious imitation, I wondered? Somehow Katherine had the air of someone who had not quite made the grade socially in the social set to which she aspired.

Looking back, it seems to me that Kitty's household had been a bit *déclassé*, something I had sensed as a child when I compared her apartment with my other cousins' households. Lloyd and Louise had never had aspired to more, but it rather looked as if Katherine had made the attempt but hadn't quite made the grade.

Reluctantly, we left the cozy little apartment and walked back through the June sunlight to the vastness of the Big House. Once we got there, we went our several ways. I lost track of the others in that vastness. Evidently, they had returned to whatever they had been doing last time they were there.

Left alone again, I first just wandered around. The immensity of the place appalled me, and I was reluctant to start anything at all for fear of being swallowed up. Presently, I came upon Louise and Katherine in a corner of a downstairs hall going through letters.

Both were sitting on wooden crates, Louise with a look of excited discovery on her face, Katherine almost aggressively, sitting with her knees apart under her wide skirt, much as Cousin Catherine had done in times past.

"Here, Russell," Katherine said. "I don't think we ought to be reading these. They are letters from your mother to Cousin Margaret during the war. This desk is full of letters, and the hall closet there is jammed to the top with boxes of papers. Most of them seem to be letters."

Louise spoke up. "Yes, and we have to go through each letter most carefully. We have found about eighty dollars in cash hidden away in envelopes, in nickels and dimes and occasional dollar bills. I guess she must have sold some garden produce, squirreled away the proceeds, and forgotten them."

I stood looking over the packet of letters Katherine had given me. They contained the usual trivia of family correspondence, news twenty years old of long-forgotten colds, comments on the weather, the garden, a minor triumph of mine at school, sympathy over Cousin Margaret's wartime financial travails. Gripped by the mania for preservation that seemed to characterize the house, I hesitated to throw them away; they were from the war, and war was history was it not? And yet of what practical value were they? Putting off making a decision, I laid them down on the edge of the desk and looked around the room.

The red marble living room mantel clock still regarded me forlornly from the floor in the center of the hall. Around it were stacks of newspapers, neatly tied with string. I looked into the closet opposite. As my cousins had said, it contained boxes of business and legal papers, but it also contained more bundles of newspapers and magazines.

Briefly, I glanced at the *New York Times* headline that had caught my attention the day before and, with difficulty, restrained the temptation to lose myself in the details of General Patton's meteoric advances across France and Germany and my own minor part in it.

The temptation was strong; I had *lived* those events, but never *read about them* except in the *Stars and Stripes*, hardly the world's greatest newspaper. Among the magazines were the *Saturday Evening Post* for May 1, 1935, the *Literary Digest* of fatal prognostication for December 1932, and *Cosmopolitan*, June 1933. Just old enough to be fascinating reading.

Actually, this business of wandering through rooms and opening drawers and closets at random became a real problem. The collection was so varied and so fascinating that we found ourselves trapped by our own curiosity. It was like an endless Christmas. While each of us was engaged in unpacking some little area, we would be interrupted by a cry of, "Look what I found" from elsewhere in the house. We would all rush toward the voice, becoming involved in unpacking or unwrapping the newest series of discoveries and forgetting all about the work we had originally started.

Our discoveries ran the gamut from the valuable to the ridiculous. We found bundles of sealing wax, old-fashioned mechanical pencils, and chips and counting devices from games apparently once popular but now unknown to us.

One of the more pathetic was a Victorian ear horn made of something like tortoiseshell, an acoustic device used in pre-electrical days to aid the deaf. In my youth, an old man or woman calling out "Eh? Eh?" with their horn to an ear was a figure of fun. Thinking of Cousin Margaret, the fun went out of it, and it became simply pathetic.

Early on, we learned to laugh, however. "We can either laugh our way or cry our way through all this," we used to say. "Crying our way through leads to madness." Hackneyed though it may sound, it was true, for what we were doing was exhuming and disposing of an entire family's history, a family that was our own.

Other findings involved little machines characteristic of the Victorian infatuation with the mechanical, from a time when Great Exhibitions were built on the marvels of the new manufacturing age, many of which did not work very well. We found one, an intricate desk machine for making staples out of plain wire.

It was all one operation. One fed in a roll of wire and operated the machine by punching a handle that both made the staple and affixed it to the paper. Another of those Victorian gadgets that did not quite work, though the basic idea was good for its time.

Many of these little items were of minimal value but often caught our fancy. Early in the summer, we each acquired a peach basket and, as we unpacked these little trinkets, we would put them in our own peach basket. At the end of the day, we would compare our finds, and if no one objected they were ours. I stored mine in a closet and sent them to "Early Clutter," my abortive antique venture.

"Peach basketing" became an accepted word in the lexicon of Open Country. As the summer wore on, however, the items in the peach baskets increased in value in a covert competition that was a harbinger of the bitterness at summer's end.

Because it took some time for us to realize the enormity of the task, it seemed to increase in size as we unpacked. When I first arrived, I expected to spend two weeks. At the end of a week's work, I realized that at least three weeks of work remained. After a second week of work, my estimate increased to four *more* weeks, and so on. I finally spent more than four months there.

My home and business on the West Coast receded from my mind. When asked if I did not miss my "real" life, I replied that it was like asking a drowning man if he misses land, a man so involved in keeping his head above water that he cannot remember what dry land is like. Not the least of my problems was my West Coast lover who, despite a trip East to assess the matter, was still not happy at my absence.

But on that first day, the newspapers represented, for me, "Square One." Faced with that amorphous enormity, I could only deal with one small detail. I decided to ask Katherine and Louise, who were still immersed in their correspondence.

"Perhaps I could help by carrying some of these newspapers outside," I said," We'll have more room in here, and there are people who buy old papers. I seem to remember seeing some newspapers in Cousin Margaret's apartment and elsewhere in the house. I don't dare stack them on a porch or anywhere in the house because they are too heavy. We can put them on the roofed brick terrace outside the living room where they will be dry in case of rain."

"Well, it would be a help to clear some of them away" was all the response I got. My cousins were again deep in wartime America, as described by my mother in her characteristically sloping handwriting. "Katherine, listen to this ..." was the last thing I heard as I went in search of further newspapers.

For the balance of the morning, while my cousins were reading letters, I sweated over old newspapers. There seemed to be stacks of them all over the house. I wandered through the rooms looking for them and carrying them down to the terrace with Lloyd's help. By the time we were through, we had amassed a stack of newspapers about five feet high and twenty feet long on the brick walk outside the living room.

While searching for newspapers, I discovered other evidence of wartime saving as well. My cousin had washed, flattened, and bundled vegetable and fruit cans. She had even removed the metal tops and bottoms from Bab-O cans (a now nonexistent cleaning powder similar to Comet), saving both them and the cylindrical cardboard containers. Having saved them, she had evidently failed to have them picked up. Or at least the last lot.

When we broke for lunch and returned to the apartment, Lloyd spoke up.

"How are we going to get those newspapers out to the garden?" Lloyd asked. "It's a long way from the house."

"Oh, Lord, you're right," I replied. "We might use a wheelbarrow, but it would take forever. What we really need is a moving van! Let's think about it for awhile. Maybe I can borrow something, perhaps a pickup."

Louise spoke up. "I don't think that would work. I've been in the garden and the ground is too soft for a truck. We don't want a truck mired in the garden on top of our other problems." I looked over at Lloyd and he shrugged.

After lunch, Lloyd and I returned to our work and, in the middle of the afternoon, we had our first break. A rumble distracted us from our work, and we went outside to see a large truck parked outside the kitchen door. A husky man in very dirty clothes dismounted from the truck and asked for "the old lady who used to live here."

Lloyd and I looked at each other. Lloyd answered. "I'm sorry, but she died last winter. Is there anything we can do for you? We are her heirs."

The man assumed a not-too-convincing air of sorrow. "I'm sorry to hear it," Abruptly, he turned businesslike. I buy junk. Name's Rubino. I used to buy old paper from the old lady from time to time. I buy old paper, rags, and old metal. There's lots of junk here I used to try to buy, but she would never let me."

Another contradiction. Cousin Margaret weeping on her knees because she could not saw a soup bone, and, at the same time, refusing to sell useless junk that might have brought her some extra comfort.

Lloyd and I looked at each other. This time, he waited for me to speak up. "Well," I said, "we have collected a lot of old newspapers. Maybe you'd like to take a look at them?"

We led him around the house to the terrace. Rubino looked at them thoughtfully. "Hm. Bundled. Can't get much for them. I'll give you three bucks for the lot. How about other things?" It was obvious that he regarded Open Country as a treasure trove.

Again, Lloyd looked at me. I began to realize that looking to others to lead off was a characteristic of his. "I think we'd better sort first," I said. "We'll get in touch with you."

I received in return a business card that appeared to have seen better days. We helped him lug the heavy bundles to the truck. The papers from the apartment were still in the garage, and, while we were carrying them out, Rubino's magpielike eyes spied a roll of copper wire.

"Give you four bits for that." Rubino gave me the $3.50 for the lot and drove away. Lloyd and I were flushed with success. Even that small accomplishment seemed large. We walked back to the apartment where Louise and Katherine were waiting. I handed the money to Louise, who laid it down on the kitchen table and looked at it with uncertainty.

"What do we do with it?" I asked.

"I don't know. Shall we split it now, or shall we accumulate it and split later?" This from Lloyd.

Katherine came decisively to the fore. "Heavens, if we split every time we make a sale we'll go mad divvying up small amounts. Why not keep it somewhere and divide when we have something worth splitting?"

Louise spoke up, "I remember seeing a china sugar canister in the Big House kitchen. It looked as if it was the last of a set. Why don't we keep it there? Not in the kitchen, of course; up here in the apartment."

Lloyd spoke up. "Louise has the small change we found around the house. Why don't we bring it all up here and keep the cash in one place?"

"Fine," I said.

Our first sale made, we each began to appreciate in concrete terms the value of what Cousin Margaret had left us, and to realize also the effect that our giant storehouse might have on outsiders.

There was no doubt that Rubino would make a profit on the many pounds of paper that we had helped him load. There was also no doubt and he was intensely curious about the house contents, and that the word would spread locally of Cousin Margaret's death and the availability of that which had not been available before.

Clearly, Rubino was itching to make offers on a great deal more than the newspapers we had sold him. The eagerness with which he had talked me out of the roll of copper wire (whose worth I could not assess) showed that he was also looking for easy money to be picked up from people who had no idea of the value of the things they were selling. It was disconcerting to realize that we would be dealing with people whose knowledge was greater than ours, and who would try to persuade us to sell things cheaply, hoping to make a profit from our ignorance.

Lloyd brought the sugar canister up from the kitchen in the Big House and placed the money in it. "I'm afraid, old man, that Louise and I must go. I know it seems early, but we have an hour and a half drive ahead of us to get back to Long Island. We generally try and leave early enough to miss the traffic. I imagine that Katherine will want to leave as well."

"Yes. I want to get back in time to get dinner on the table at a reasonable hour. It takes about an hour to get to Mt. Kisco."

"Okay," I said. "I'll lock up the house and then drive back to Tom and Dorli's. I'll be back around nine o'clock in the morning."

"By the way," added Lloyd. "Here is a set of keys for you, old man."

"Thanks," I replied.

Katherine gave me a cousinly peck on the cheek before she hurried downstairs. Louise waited a moment and then gave me an affectionate squeeze. "We're really glad you're here, Russell," she said and then bustled down the stairs.

After they had all driven away, I walked over to the Big House. The elation of our sale gone, I appreciated anew the size of the job before us. The disappearance of the huge quantity of newspapers left no gap in the house. The hall off the living room looked just as full as it had before, and the immensity of the house seemed to mock the puny efforts of the afternoon. After all that sweat, nothing seemed to have been accomplished.

I began to realize why Lloyd had sounded so discouraged in his letters. My cousins had been going through this same experience for a matter of months, and felt the same tide of discouragement that was now overtaking me. What had we done that day? I had spent much of it lugging bundles of newspapers around the house. Louise and Katherine had been rooted in the living room occupied with the minutiae of family correspondence like a pair of small-town gossips. Lloyd had put in his time cleaning out empty matchboxes, accumulated one-pound butter cartons, and similar kinds of trash from the kitchen and laundry.

Four of us had been occupied in widely separated areas of the house, out of the sight and sound of the others. Three separate and unrelated projects had been started. One, by luck, completed; the net effect was no change. Unless we three were to go mad, we must work together, taking a project at a time so that, at the end of the day, we could say to ourselves "There! *That's* done!

Where had we best begin? Somehow it seemed logical to begin at one end of one wing and to clear toward the center of the house. It also seemed that our greatest problem was the enormous amount of trash that filled the house, items that either had no resale value or, like the newspapers, could only the sold by the pound. Remembering Rubino's remark about buying rags, I walked to Cousin Margaret's former bedroom at the far end of the second floor of the bedroom wing to look at the closets.

Peering anew into the four closets and the big armoire in her bedroom and the adjacent Green Room, I learned that she had evidently never disposed of any of the dresses and coats that had hung there since Cousin Catherine was alive. Besides a flashy yellow satin dress that must have belonged to Cousin Jessie, there were several dozen cotton and wool dresses of that styleless mode of Helen Hokinson's cartoon old ladies in the *New Yorker*. With a few exceptions, the material seemed to have been ruined by damp and moths. Clearing out this room would be a tough job, but it would go fast because little sorting would be necessary. Most of it was trash.

The subject of dresses drew my mind back to the ancestral antebellum dresses in the attic that I had looked at the day before. Pulling down the disappearing stairs and climbing to the attic again, I checked the trunks more thoroughly. Opening each in turn, I found that none showed signs of damp or rot. I remembered then that Janet Alkiewicz, a friend of many years who lived in nearby Ridgefield, had once worked in the costume department of the Museum of the City of New York. I resolved to ask her over at the earliest possible moment to help us decide how to dispose of this treasure trove of history. Breathing a sigh of relief, I walked down the stairs and back to Cousin Margaret's bedroom.

On this cheerful note, I prepared to leave the house and return to Tom and Dorli's for the evening. The chill of winter was not yet off the house despite the warm sunlight we had had that day and our efforts to let the warm air in by opening as many windows as possible. As I walked through the rooms, closing windows, I became aware of a subtle change coming over the house. During the day, when it was occupied, it had an air of dejected decay. Empty now, with the setting sun blocked by the maples on all sides, it began to assume an almost menacing aspect.

I became aware of small noises, of dark shadows, and of chills in my spine. After closing three of the four French doors in the living room, I walked out the fourth to smell the blossoms of the syringa bush outside. While I was there, an errant breeze closed the door I had left open. For no good reason, it took all my courage to walk back into the living room and continue my solitary tour of inspection. Later, when I moved to Cousin Margaret's apartment and returned from late dinners, I avoided pointing my flashlight up at the windows for fear of what I might see. It was a strange sensation.

At night, the gaunt ruin of the porch, the tattered blinds at the windows, the broken shutters hanging by one hinge seemed to loom above me, menacing and awesome. And yet, in the morning, or when I had company, these imaginary dangers vanished into the thin air whence they came. 'Twas the stuff of which ghost stories are made.

The next morning, I avoided the Big House and prepared coffee for my cousins in the garage apartment, and, while I waited for them, I thought again about the dresses up in the attic and about Janet Alkiewicz. As soon as my cousins were settled, I asked them if I could invite Janet over to take a look at them on the weekend.

Katherine spoke up first. "Sure. We need all the help we can get here. If you know someone who knows something about the things in the house, by all means bring them in."

Louise was more enthusiastic. "Oh, Russell, "she said, "of course ask her over. With her experience, I am sure she will be able to help us in many ways. There are a number of things in the Big House I would like to know more about." Lloyd merely smiled and nodded his head at me, as usual following others' leads. I did not know it then, but this short conversation prepared the way for one of the most pleasant and productive experiences we had that summer.

Having gotten that settled, I proceeded to my second agenda item. "Fine. In the meantime, I have a second suggestion to make. It seems to me that, instead of working in different parts of the house doing different things, maybe if we concentrated on one area we would have more of a feeling of getting things done. If we could get, say, one room done, we could at least point to one part of the house with a feeling of completion. What do you think?"

"That makes sense, old man," Lloyd replied. "I remember when we first started, Katherine and Louise worked only in the servants' wing, and, whereas it doesn't look it because Quinn wouldn't let us throw anything out, we did get those bedrooms cleared out of a lot of trash. That's where all those bales of stuff in the servants' dining room came from."

"That reminds me. I was looking at the vegetable garden last night. I wonder if we might think of burning trash out there?" I asked. "Paying Matt or someone else to drag it off to the dump is obviously too expensive, and there is a probably a charge for dumping anyway."

Lloyd brightened a bit, and then a worried look came over his face. "Quite right. Matt told us it cost three dollars to dump the stuff he took away before. But wouldn't burning be dangerous? Flying sparks and all?"

"Not if we waited for a rainy day. Once the house roofs are wet, it wouldn't make any difference. When we have finished burning the backlog, we could have a small fire every day or so. I'll bet there is a roll of chicken wire in the barn, and if we put that over a small fire, there'll be little danger of sparks." I remembered that that was how we used to burn trash at Lacey Green.

Katherine spoke up. "I don't see why there shouldn't be a roll of chicken of chicken wire somewhere about." She snorted. "We have everything else, it seems." Then, more seriously, "My son, Bill, has an Indian pump. I could bring that, and I'll bet Bill would come and help as well."

"What's an Indian pump?" I asked

"It's a tank. Holds about ten gallons of water. There's a little hand-operated pump and a hose so you can spray the water," was the reply.

"How are we going to get the trash out to the garden?" Lloyd wanted to know. "It's a long way from the house."

That brought us back to the earlier discussion about transporting trash out to the garden, a problem to which none of us had any solution. On that discouraging note, we walked over to the Big House. Katherine and Louise returned to the open chest of letters they had been reading the day before.

"You know," Katherine said as she sat down, setting her hat on a nearby crate, "this room really doesn't look any different from the way it did yesterday. All those papers and magazines are gone, and we didn't make a dent in the place." She picked up another letter.

"That's what I meant earlier, Katherine. Unless we all concentrate in one room, we aren't going to get anyplace. Why don't we start on one room and do a room at a time, all together?" I asked.

Katherine put down her letter. "Might be worth trying. We did it in the servants' wing, but that was easy because most of it was trash. We didn't have to store anything. We just brought it down in bundles and left it in the servants' dining room. Where would you suggest we begin?"

"Cousin Margaret's bedroom," I said. "It's at the end of this wing, and we might begin there and work our way down to the main hall, doing a room at a time. Then at least there would be one room, and finally one wing, done and complete. I was up there last night looking through closets and things. Much of the clothing is gone to rags. Maybe some of the things could be saved, but not much."

Louise spoke up. "If there is anything worthwhile, could I have it for my church? I mean, if it isn't valuable but could be used by someone. We have a sewing group and we take old clothing and fix it up to give away to people who need it."

"If it's all right with Katherine, I'm sure I have no objection," I said. "I hate to see things wasted. Why don't you two decide what can be salvaged, and Lloyd and I will take charge of dragging the trash outside."

Katherine snorted. "Pretty sneaky of you to get out of making decisions. But I've no objection to giving away old clothing. Let's get to work."

We four walked up to Cousin Margaret's bedroom. Katherine strode over to a closet and swung the door wide. She picked a dress at random off the rack and looked at it. "Heavens," she said, "I haven't seen a dress like this in years." She held it up to herself. "No style. I'm glad I wasn't an old lady in those years." Disengaging it from the wooden hanger, she flung it onto the bed, where its many ruffles settled down in a disordered heap.

Louise pounced on it. "Why, its voile. Beautiful material." She tested it expertly with a fingernail. "Rotten though. No use to keep it." She dropped it to the floor. The two women worked swiftly for a few minutes, pulling dresses out of the closet and dumping most of them on the floor. Only a few linen prints stayed on the bed. The rest lay in a pile on the floor where they were beginning to get in the way.

Lloyd looked at the pile with distaste. "I say, old man, how are we going to get this downstairs? We can't take them down by the armful. I'm not as young as you are, and I don't want to climb those stairs any more than I have to."

Louise spoke up immediately. "Oh, Lloyd, you remember that big pile of curtains in the linen closet? We used them to bundle up the trash in the servants' wing. There are lots of them left, and we can use them here." Louise returned to consideration of a black silk dress generously embroidered with jet.

"Funeral clothes." This from Katherine. "The Leverich sisters were famous for them. Turning up at family funerals wearing weeds dating from their mother's death. Complete with veils."

Lloyd and I walked to the linen closet. I opened the door and stood back, appalled. Floor to ceiling, the shelves were full. Linen sheets, bath towels, face towels, linen brocade tablecloths—each in neat, categorical piles. Delicate little finger-bowl doilies, tea napkins, embroidered cloths for breakfast trays. The well-stocked linen closet of a bygone era. Lloyd spoke up. "That's not the worst." He flung open two adjacent closets and a large wooden chest nearby. "Here. See here."

Three linen closets. And all of them full to the brim. How were we ever to get through it all? "Here," he said, indicating another chest, "are the curtains Louise was talking about."

I reached down into the chest and pulled out a curtain. It was printed linen, sturdy but sun-faded, and at least twelve feet long.

Not made for the eight-foot ceilings in today's apartments but perfect for our purpose. Dump the trash in the center, hold the corners together—and we'd have perfect sacks for carrying or dragging.

"There are dozens of them," Lloyd said. "One thing about this family, they didn't stint on quantity. Bought everything by the dozen. Good quality too."

"Saved them by the dozen, too."

"Quite right, old man," he replied drily.

Together, we carried a bundle of curtains back and started to wrap up the dresses and other things that Katherine and Louise had rejected.

"What a pity," Louise was saying as I walked into the room, "I can't get the stopper out of this cologne bottle." She held it out for me to look at. It was a bottle of Guerlain Imperiale, stopper stuck, the label faded with age.

"I remember seeing those bottles when I was a child. Up in the attic," I said. "They went to Europe sometime in the nineties and brought back a lot of cologne and French scented soap. I remember Cousin Margaret showing me some bottles of this in a trunk in the attic. Never been opened. The Guerlain seal was still over the stopper."

We were interrupted by a strangled sound from the dressing room.

"Dahlings!"

Katherine appeared in the doorway, an enormous feather boa draped around her shoulders, a tortoise and ostrich fan held before her like a Ziegfeld Follies dancer. We stood transfixed at the sight. Laughing, her point made, she tossed the boa down on a pile of rejects, a small cloud of ostrich feathers following in its wake.

"The boa is all dried out, but this fan is in pretty good shape. What do we do with it? And there is a drawerful of fans there. Mostly painted and lace fans."

Louise bustled into the dressing room, magnifying glass in hand. Her voice floated out to us through the door.

"Oh, but these are beautiful. Look, here is one Cousin Catherine carried at her coming-out in 1894."

"Yes, I was looking at them when Lloyd came in yesterday. Every one of the fans is labeled. She knew where each of them had been used, and by whom."

"But what do we do with them?" Louise asked. "They are too beautiful to throw away, but people don't use fans anymore." Quite right, I thought, more's the pity. When I was young, many older women were so skilled in their use that their fans became a way of expressing their personalities.

I remembered that Cousin Julie had always carried one of intricately carved sandalwood that scented the air with it, a pleasant odor I had called "The Cousin Julie Smell" when I was little. It was always fluttering in her hand—except when she wanted to conclude a statement or a story. The sound of her fan snapping shut always accompanied some emphatic point she wanted to make.

I thought again of Janet Alkiewicz.

"Well," said Katherine, "while we are waiting for your friend Janet, why don't we set aside part of this built-in closet and keep all the fans here? I'm sure we'll find more somewhere in the house." The look on her face indicated that, in this house, we were likely to find most anything—or everything.

"Oh my, yes," Louise said breathlessly, "I remember seeing some in a desk in the living room, and I'm sure there will be more in the trunks upstairs. I'll take care of the labeling. That could be important." Katherine had an "I told you so" look on her face.

We worked there for the balance of the day—Katherine and Louise sorting and discarding, Lloyd and I dragging discards down to the porch by the front door where they would be out of the way but protected from the rain. The variety was enormous, starting with close-fitting hats ornamented with jet. (This brought to mind the proverbial Boston ladies again. When asked by a stylish New

York woman "Where on earth do you buy your hats?" they'd reply, "We don't buy our hats, we have our hats.")

There were fur coats, cloth coats with fur collars and cuffs, a wide variety of dresses in wool, fur muffs, silk and cotton garments heavily ornamented with embroidery, cologne bottles half-full, hatboxes and dress boxes bearing the names of familiar stores that had long since moved from the locations shown on their labels.

Some indeed were once well-known and now closed (A. J. Stewarts, that used to compete with Wanamakers down on nearby Tenth Street was one). There were kid gloves by the dozen, none of them large enough to fit a child more than ten years old today, and an enormous variety of long, black cotton lisle stockings.

"Why all those cotton stockings," I asked Louise once. "Didn't they wear silk?"

"Oh, Russell," she replied, "in those days ladies never wore silk stockings. Only the"—she paused momentarily, looking at me over her half-lenses—"other ladies." I got the point.

The items we saved were indeed exquisite. There was a whole drawerful of fans; a diaphanous stole of sheerest chiffon ornamented at each end with bright glass beads, two white wool opera cloaks lined with figured silk and trimmed with heavy embroidery and cloisonné buttons, and Cousin Jessie's bright yellow dress.

"I know the top looks as if it belonged in a circus, with all the gold braid and sequins," Louise explained, "but the skirt is gorgeous embroidered silk. I couldn't bear to throw it away. Someone ought to be able to use it."

"Lloyd," she added, "would you and Russell take that pile of things down to the car? Katherine and I felt we might try to save them, that is, my church group. You don't mind, do you, Russell? You said it was all right." Louise looked a little hesitant.

"Good heavens no, Anything to see them put to use."

Lloyd and I made a few trips down with the church items, and then we all congregated in Cousin Margaret's apartment. After

Lloyd and I had loaded the station wagon, he pulled a small paper bag out of the glove compartment.

"Louise and I thought we'd supply a little something to help us relax at the end of the day," he said. "I drink scotch, and Katherine drinks bourbon. I hope you drink one or the other?" Lloyd looked hopeful, like a small child who wants to be sure he has got the lesson right.

"Scotch, and how very kind of you. What about Louise?"

"She doesn't drink because she usually drives. I drive if we bring up the Sunbeam Talbot, but I won't drive the station wagon. Automatic drive, you know, old fellow." Lloyd lifted his lip a little scornfully.

"I'm like you. I drive a Porsche myself." As a matter of fact, I still do. Bought new and still going strong more than 260,000 miles later.

Together, we walked up to the apartment. Lloyd disappeared into the kitchen and reappeared shortly with three drinks. Katherine, he, and I settled down to relax while Louise got herself a cup of coffee.

"If you don't mind, old man, we won't be up over the weekend. We three usually work Monday to Friday and then tend to our home chores on the weekend. We don't have enough energy left over at the end of the day to do anything when we get back, and we need the weekend to collect ourselves. You won't be lonely, will you?" Lloyd asked.

"Not at all. I have a lot of friends in the area I can get in touch with. I hope you won't mind if I show them through the place? I thought I'd get in touch with Janet, who lives nearby. Then I have a friend in New York, a cabinetmaker who used to work for the Metropolitan and has some interior decorator friends and antique contacts. He might have some ideas."

"Louise and I don't mind if Katherine doesn't. Lord knows the more ideas we can get about this place, the better."

Katherine spoke up. "Of course I don't mind. We're going to

have to find a way of disposing of it sometime, and we might as well begin now." My cousins and I sat around chatting for a short while, and then they left, leaving me to lock up the place. I moved quickly through this task, for the oppressive mood was on the house again, and I had a real desire to get out of the house and away before it grew stronger.

On my return to Tom and Dorli's, I phoned both Janet and my friend Allen Matlock, in New York. Janet was interested and agreed to meet me in the house the next morning. I really looked forward to her visit because I had not seen her since I had graduated from Harvard some thirteen years before. Allen said that he would love a day in the country and would drive up with a friend on Sunday.

I looked forward to seeing him, too, for I had not seen him since my early days in New York after graduation when, as a young newspaperman, I was wrestling with the pangs of accepting the fact that I was gay. He was a good and supportive friend at that time, but with a funny set of values.

I had met him first in a gay bar. I liked him, and we talked for some time. During the conversation, I asked him what he did for a living. "I'm a carpenter," was the reply. I later doubted that because, when we shook hands in parting, I noted that his hands were smooth and soft. Not at all the hands of a workman. Actually, he was an administrator for Gimbel's department store. He told me later that, with so many snobs around, telling people he was a carpenter was a kind of test. People who were put off by the "fact" that he was a workman were not worth knowing, he said. Actually, he *was* a very good carpenter, having made much of the cabinetry in his apartment himself.

I did not know it, but those two phone calls opened up what was, for me, perhaps the pleasantest aspect of the entire summer. Many friends came that summer to visit me and to see the house. Each of them, in their own way, made a signal contribution, they all gave something of themselves to us and made our task easier. This was in sharp contrast to our experiences with those who wanted to buy from us. The formers' freewill gifts stand out in my mind in sharp contrast with the greed of those with whom we tried to deal—greed that created a rift between Katherine on the one hand and Lloyd, Louise, and myself on the other much later. Greed, too, perhaps, that led me into a business venture I was not prepared to deal with.

CHAPTER 5

That Nameless Thump

Besides Tom and Dorli, I had a number of friends in the neighborhood of Open Country. Some, like Tom, I had met elsewhere; others I had known from my youth in Ridgefield and Wilton. Janet Alkiewicz was one of the former. I had met her first in New York through mutual friends and had invited her up to Harvard College several times in the days before I actively accepted my own gayness. As a matter of fact, she had come to my graduation when I was under the impression that I was in love with her. It wasn't difficult. Janet is a very lovable woman.

Shortly after that, she had connected with another friend, Andrzej Alkiewicz, a refugee from Poland whom I had met indirectly through the unlikely offices of a canon at the Cathedral of St. John the Divine in New York.

Father West, or "Fazzer West" as his brood called him, had sponsored no fewer than seven young men, displaced persons, who were unable to return to their native Poland when it went Communist after the war. Each of these gentlemen, one with the tongue-twisting name of Benon Przybielski (The first four letters are pronounced "Pshi," a combination that does not come easily to tongues accustomed to English), had, in turn, been sponsored by one of the seven Houses at Harvard. The university picked up the tab for food, lodging, and tuition for the men, and the House Committees in the each house helped guide them through the mysteries of the college administration. I had come to know Ben in that latter connection.

Benon had led me to Father West, and he in turn had led me to Andrjez. As a matter of fact, it was I who had introduced Janet and Andrzej, a fact that nettled me to no end at the time of their engagement.

Janet and Andrzej had ended up living in Ridgefield, Connecticut—about five miles or so from Open Country on what was called "West Mountain." From my current perspective, the name seems a little enthusiastic since it is less than a thousand feet in height, but I only began to question the term after I visited the West and learned what real mountains looked like. West Mountain was the only mountain I had ever seen until I traveled west with my parents in 1934 and learned what "real" mountains were like.

I had more or less kept track of Janet via Christmas cards after I had moved west eight years before, so I knew how to get in touch with her in Ridgefield. Shortly after my arrival, I called her, and she was enthusiastic in her welcome. In addition, she swiftly arranged to come over to Open Country on the Saturday morning shortly after my call.

When she arrived, I found her just as lovable as she had been more than ten years before. She was, and still, is a short woman, a little inclined to plumpness, with a chubby implike face and a perky retroussé nose that wrinkles when she laughs, naturally curly dark brown hair, and mischievous eyes. Behind it all lies an excellent mind and an intensely sophisticated view of the world, a product of her association with her grandfather, who was a scholar of note. I have recently seen a current photograph of her, and she is much the same. A little plumper and with gray hair, but the rest is still there. How genuinely unchanged we are as we grow older! Some intrinsic self always remains, despite outer changes.

I showed her through the house, and then we went up to look over the contents of the trunks. It was not necessary to go up to the unlighted part of the attic—in various bedrooms, we had found a number of trunks containing antique dresses, lace-edged linen, and cotton underclothing (of a design so old-fashioned that we could not tell what use many of them served). We figured that many of these trunks had been brought down from the attic to save the contents when the roof in the front of the house began to fail. There were still a few trunks in that part of the attic, however, that had remained dry over the years.

When I opened the first one, I noticed something I had not seen before—each trunk bore a label inside the lid showing the history of the dresses stored there, testifying again to the care with which Cousin Margaret had preserved the past. Janet's eyes sparkled with delight when we unwrapped the first item from its tissue paper covering, a dress that brought back wartime memories for me.

Black velvet with an antique lace high collar, puffed sleeves, a sweeping bell-like skirt, and a slight train, the dress also sported a matching black velvet hat with plumes in the style that Mae West made famous, but without her lush slovenliness. Dramatic, but in flawless taste—pure Charles Dana Gibson or, perhaps, pure *My Fair Lady* for those of more recent vintage.

This dress, however, had a lot more to offer in terms of presenting the "essential woman" than did the Edwardian china-doll prettiness presented by Audrey Hepburn in the racetrack scene.

It bore a label that read, "Black Velvet with Lace Collar/ Made by Delacroix in Vienna for Catherine in 1893, lined with red silk. (Black velvet lined with red silk must have been stunning, I thought.) Made over by Mme. Albert in New York in 1900 and relined."

I remembered the dress well, for it had been featured in a British War Relief pageant in 1940. It had been modeled then by a tall, pretty, stately girl with dark hair and a high bust who gave the costume, with its pinched waist that accentuated the bosom above, sex appeal without cheapness.

Remembering my grossly overweight cousin, it seemed strange to realize that she had once herself been that slim and stately and probably very attractive to men as well. Given a picture of older people, it is always a shock to try to imagine them when they were young. What strength of character Aunt Annie must have had to keep that one under wraps! Not for nothing was she known as one of New York's magisterial matriarchs.

Janet was breathless as she examined the dress and matching hat. She ran her hands over its silky softness with almost reverent hands, admiring its pristine beauty. "Beautiful," she murmured to herself. "Simply beautiful. They knew how to dress in those days, didn't they?"

"Yes," I said, thinking to myself of the pedestal on which women had been placed in that age. Truly, the dress was made to render a woman both desirable and aloof. The classic Gibson Girl look that has not been matched since.

The next label was much less dramatic and more nostalgic in tone. "Pretty white silk party dress worn at balls and gay parties by C. in 1895–6." It was a far simpler dress, made of white silk and worn off-the-shoulder with a modest white lace bertha covering the bosom. Very demure, very Victorian. By 1895, my little cousin had been going deaf for eleven years, and I wondered how many times she had wistfully seen her older sister off to parties she could no longer enjoy because of her increasing deafness. Again, I thought of the pain she must have suffered during those wasted years of her youth, when she must have indeed been a wallflower, able only to watch others dancing from the sidelines.

We looked at a few more dresses, and then Janet sat back and brushed an errant curl behind her ear. "Russell, what luck. There is a perfect mine of old dresses here and every one of them labeled. If you'd like, I'll get in touch with Isabelle Miller at the Museum of the City of New York. I used to work under her, you know, and she is always looking for dresses worn by old New York families. They are in beautiful condition, and the fact that they are labeled will make her even more interested." Janet sat back, breathless, and gazed at me with a broad smile on her face.

I was delighted at the prospect. "Do you suppose you could help us unpack them? My cousins and I know very little about taking care of costumes, and perhaps you could arrange and catalog them for us. Then you could get in touch with Miss Miller; you could give her a better idea of what we have to offer her."

Janet's eyes betrayed her eagerness, but she looked serious. "I'd love to. It would be like going back to work at the Museum again. I loved the work there and was sorry to leave. I can't come on the weekends, when Andrzej is home, but during the week I could come over during the day while Caroline is in the house taking care of the children. I have two, you know, eight-year-old Maria and the baby, Christopher."

"Yes, you told me about them in one of your letters." I thought for a minute, anxious to avoid putting off her kind offer. "I'll have to ask my cousins about it, but I am sure they would be happy for the expert help. Why don't I phone you Monday after I've talked to them?"

"Wonderful. And in the meantime, why not come to dinner tonight? We're having a couple of friends in. Bennet and Jordy Jack. Do you know them? Bennet used to be Bennet Pierrepont."

Did I know Bennet!

Bennet and I went back a long way. Bennet had lived in Ridgefield when I was a child, though I did not know her at that time. Sometime during the war, my father ran across Mary Jay, a woman who was a descendent of John Jay, the first Chief Justice of the Supreme Court of the United States. They had a similar interest in genealogy, and through their investigations, they discovered out that he and Miss Jay were cousins.

She was a direct descendent of John Jay. *He*, and therefore I, were descendants of John Jay's sister, a woman who had eloped with the Reverend Harry Munro. They had had several children, of whom my ancestor was one. For some reason, now lost in the mists of antiquity, she had refused to marry the good reverend, or at least there is no record of such a marriage, and thus it would appear that there is the "stain of bastardy" in my background. Of course, there was much laughter about the matter, and I have always thought it strange that a minister would live with a woman who refused to marry him. It must have been interesting then, and I wish I could step back in time and learn the whole story.

In any case, Miss Jay had a cousin who lived in Ridgefield, a Mrs. Pierrepont. Bennet Pierrepont was her granddaughter. I never knew the former, but I rather imagine she was a *grande dame* in the traditional manner, and I also suspect that Bennet modeled herself after her grandmother.

Quite by accident, when I was at Harvard after the war, Bennet and I had crossed paths and made cousinly contact. She was a sensual young women, rather given to being grand, but amusingly rather than offensively so. She played the role of the *grande dame*, as she has always done since, and she played it well. She had red hair and the complexion that went with it and a lush body, and she was given to wearing green, which set off her red hair to perfection.

She was wearing one such flowing watered silk number without straps at one of the Waltz Evenings for which Boston was famous, and was my date for the evening. Since both she and I loved to waltz, we spent a great deal of the time on the dance floor, and once, as we passed our table, those sitting out that dance arose and pointed dramatically at her.

We were both puzzled, but on the next round, we realized that they were pointing at her back. It seemed that, in waltzing, I had managed to open the zipper that held her dress together, and that the only thing holding her dress together was my hand across her back! It was also at this same dance that a friend of hers came up to the table and handed her a five dollar bill (a considerable sum in those days) across the table with the remark, "This is for last night. Thank you." Evidently it involved payment for a taxi the previous night, but other interpretations were placed on it immediately; she and I laughed about it for years.

After I graduated from Harvard, I lost track of her. Some fifteen years later, when I was living in Los Angeles, I had received a telegram:

Coming to Canoga Park (a suburb of Los Angeles) to stay with Jordy's cousins. Can I see you too?
    Bennet P. Jack

Jack? I knew no one by the name of Jack. "Bennet?" Bennet P.? And who was this "Jordy?" Did I know this man? Or was it someone trying to get in touch with the producer, Ross Hunter, whose letters and phone calls I received from time to time? I recall one such occasion when Mr. Hunter had apparently engaged in some "casting couch" activity with a young woman and then had not followed through in the way she expected. She was angry, and it took considerable effort on my part to convince her that I was not the man she was angry with.

Carefully, I wrote my reply, expressing my happiness at hearing from "Bennet Jack" and suggesting that "Bennet Jack" phone me on arrival. I tried to make it sound as if I knew who it was, but it didn't fool Bennet for a minute. She did not allow me to forget that letter for years.

Turned out it was Bennet Pierrepont, who had married and had a son, Michael, divorced, and remarried. Lovable nut that she is, she is one of those people who falls in and out of a person's life with complete ease, and with whom it is possible to pick up again as if you had seen her only the day before.

She talked a lot about "Jordy" during our visit, but, typically, said nothing I could hang a description on. Finally, it appeared that I would meet him. I was very curious about meeting a man who would take on Bennet on a full-time basis. My last memory of the visit was of carrying a sleeping Michael onto the plane when she left to return to the East Coast. I had not seen her since. My rediscovery was to provide me with large dividends.

It seemed that Bennet was, apparently, back in my life again, and I replied to Janet's question about dinner.

"I'd love to come to dinner. I used to know Bennet when I was in college. What time?" I decided to leave out the story of her Los Angeles visit. I was sure it would come up at dinner, with embellishments. Bennet is a dramatic *raconteuse.*

"Six. We eat early because of the children."

"Fine. I'll be there at six."

I had never been to her house, and she gave me long and complex directions on how to get there. When I arrived, I found a large, rambling house on a hill surrounded by spreading lawns. The house had a substantial view, probably at least five miles wide, and I felt less shut in than I had elsewhere.

When I arrived at Andrjez and Janet's, Bennet and Jordy were already there. As the door opened, I heard Bennet's lazy Southern drawl float upstairs from Janet and Andrej's sunken living room, coupled with a deep, resonant voice not familiar to me. When I got downstairs, I found that it belonged to Jordy, a mountain of a man exuding cheerful good humor and decisiveness in every move that he made. Quite, I decided, a match for Bennet.

Also present was Janet and Andrjez's daughter, Maria, whom I had met several years before. Andrjez had brought her to the West Coast several years before when she was a very little girl and he was on a business trip, and they had stayed with me. She had been a delightful child, and I had spent an enjoyable day at Disneyland with them both. I found she was now ten and still delightful.

Also present was Andrjez's father, whom they all called "Dja-dja," a nickname for Grandfather. Sometime during the previous ten years, Andrjez had traveled to Poland and had brought his father out. Quite how he managed to do it I never learned. Since he had spent the war years in Poland under the Nazis, he had evidently learned to survive, and I surmised that there was a story there, but I never learned it.

Over cocktails and dinner, Janet talked with enthusiasm of the trunks of dresses she had looked at, and Bennet asked innumerable questions about Open Country and its contents. It began to appear that Jordy had a special interest in, as well as considerable knowledge of, American antiques of the Colonial period.

When we returned to the living room and coffee was served, Bennet made a suggestion.

"Why don't we go over and take a look for ourselves? Would you mind, Russell?" she asked.

"Not at all." Then, remembering my fears of my first evening there, "You might feel a few ghosts."

"Me, afraid?" Bennet laughed. To Janet, "Could Maria come with us?"

"Could I? Please, Mother."

"If Uncle Russell doesn't mind."

All of us—the Jacks, Janet, Andrzej and Maria, Andrzej's father, and I—piled into the Jacks' station wagon and drove over to Open Country.

In the harsh light of the old-fashioned frosted globes and in the flickering light of flashlights, the house looked even more bleak than in daylight. Our little group was swallowed up in the house. We lost one another, found one other, and were lost again in the vast tangle of rooms, like so many Tom Sawyers in the cave. The flickering flashlights were like so many fireflies in the darkened rooms, and squeals of delight resounded through the house as my various guests found things that interested or delighted them. In a macabre kind of way, the house appeared to take on life.

Maria led her grandfather through the house by the hand, exclaiming over little bits and pieces of bric-a-brac dear to children. Andrzej was appalled by the decay but expressed interest in photographing the house. It seemed that photography was his hobby, and he told me that he was fascinated by the idea of photographing "Zis noble ruin."

Bennet poked into trunks and into the fan closet, while Jordy went through the house alone, examining each piece of furniture carefully with his flashlight. Finally, he approached me.

"Russell, I'd like to come back in the daylight and take another look. You have a lot of Victorian stuff here, and there are a few pieces that might be collector's items. I can't be sure in this light, but some of them might be really valuable."

He led me upstairs to the satinwood Federal bureau with the bowed front. "If the brass handles are original, I'd be willing to pay three hundred dollars for this piece alone. And that big mirror in the downstairs hall near the living room, if you can find the finial, it might bring as much as a thousand dollars."

"What is a finial?"

"Russell, do you see the top of the mirror where the two curlicues come together?"

I had not really taken note of them. "Yes."

"Well, there is a centerpiece missing there. It was probably originally gilded, and might be either a phoenix bird or perhaps an eagle. In any case, it would complete the design."

I looked. Sure enough, the mirror, now that I looked carefully, did seem a bit unfinished.

"Of course you can come back. I had no idea we had this kind of thing in the house. My cousins and I were under the impression that it was mostly junk."

"I don't have a job now. Could I come Monday?"

"Sure. My cousins will be there then. I am sure they'd like to hear what you have to say." Sobered by Jordy's remarks, I paid careful attention to locking up before climbing back into the Jacks' car for the return trip to Janet and Andrzej's house.

The following morning, Allen Matlock and a friend, John Wainwright, came up for their promised visit. It was good to see Allen again. I had met Allen shortly after graduating from college, when I was exploring gay New York, and I had known him for about a decade. In years past, when my mother was alive, I had flown east each year for Christmas and had seen him every year. I had not, however, done that since she had died four years before, and our contact had been only by letter and Christmas card.

Wainwright was older than either of us, a weather-beaten man with a lined face, gray hair, and glasses. He appeared to be a man I could trust, but at the same time I was aware that, after he had shaken my hand, he was looking around at the house in a shrewdly appraising manner. His reaction to the house was different from that of my other friends who had come to visit.

We had a picnic lunch on the lawn in front of the house under the maples, something that became somewhat of a tradition with new visitors that summer, the house being too gloomy. Afterward, Wainwright wandered through the house by himself while Allen and I caught up with our lives. When we came to discuss Wainwright, Allen told me that he ran a small antique shop in Greenwich Village, where Allen then lived.

"Well," Allen said, "not really an antique shop. Actually, it is rather more a glorified junk shop, but his customers think they are buying antiques, so it amounts to the same thing. If something is old, it is an antique. You'd be amazed at the money junk will bring if it is displayed right."

"Hey," Wainwright called from the front porch. "What is this stuff doing here?"

I looked over and saw that he was pointing at a pile of things we had tossed out of the house, things that had appeared to have no value. "Junk," I said. "We put it there so that we could drag it out and burn it on the first rainy day. We have an Indian pump, and we want to be sure that we don't start any fires."

"Man," was the reply, "you are sitting on a fortune here, and you don't know it. Were you going to burn this?" He held up a pair of cotton lisle stockings. "Or this?" He pointed at a Dobbs hatbox from the twenties. "Or these?" This time, he held up the box of cologne bottles with the stuck tops.

"Don't you know there are collectors who will pay big bucks for such things? There almost isn't a thing in that house that won't sell."

"Even the old crocks in the cellar and the cookie molds in the kitchen?"

"Yes, damn it, yes. I haven't got the space or the money to handle this, but I wish I could. I could make a mint off this place. You have thousands of things in there, and every one of them will sell. At least *I* could sell them in my place.

Wainwright went on. "Did you know you had a lot of old dolls in a trunk in the attic? I daren't unpack them, but they looked very old indeed. Have you any idea where they came from?"

"They probably were Cousin Margaret's and Cousin Catherine's things from their childhood. Let's see now. Cousin Margaret was born in 1876, and she was the youngest. Cousin Catherine must have been born a few years before, so they probably date from at least the seventies and eighties. Maybe they saved some of their mother's dolls as well. I don't know."

"Do you know there are people who specialize in collecting dolls? You can get up to a hundred dollars *apiece* for those things. Sometimes more. Do you *know* what you have here?"

"No, not really. But I am beginning to learn."

"I hope you are living here."

"No. I'm staying with friends in Wilton. I lock up carefully at the end of the day, of course, but there is no one else here except for some tenants who live down by the barns. Anyway, you can't see the Big House from where they live."

Wainwright snorted. "What good would they do?" he asked.

"Come to think of it, I don't suppose they'd ever even hear anyone up here."

"Well," Wainwright went on, "I suggest you move into that little apartment above the greenhouse over there. With your car parked outside the Big House and perhaps a few lights in an upstairs bedroom or two, maybe you could fool the casual prowler into staying away. Do you have a phone?"

"No. Cousin Margaret was stone deaf, and she never had any reason to put one in."

"Better get one. How would you get the police here if you *did* hear someone late at night? You'll need one for other things too."

"Like what?" I was curious.

"Like calling dealers. You've got a big job here. It'll take you at least six months. You may not know it, but you are in a business. Or do you and your cousins plan to split everything even and go your ways?"

"I doubt it. I live on the West Coast, and shipping my share would be madness. And besides, I live in a four-room house." Suddenly, the hugeness of the problem hit me anew. "Lloyd and Louise have a four-room house on Long Island, and Katherine tells me her house is up for sale. We haven't really discussed it, but I strongly suspect they will want to sell as much as possible."

"Then you've got yourself a business. You've got to organize yourself. Learn what you've got and what it's worth, or you'll get the back teeth cheated off you. That stuff you have out on the porch ready to be thrown out. I could have begged it off you easily. 'You don't want this old stuff, do you? Let me have it,' I could have said, and then turned around and sold it for real money in New York. If you hadn't been a friend of Allen's, I might have done just that. Wise up!"

Wainwright paused for breath, and I stared at him, speechless. The Leverich habit of saving might pay off after all, in ways they never expected. Nor we, either, I reflected.

"Could you work with us and help us out?" I asked.

"'Fraid not. For one thing, I don't know enough, though I can see you have some really salable merchandise."

This was the first time I had thought of Cousin Margaret's belongings as *merchandise*. Family belongings were family belongings to be inherited, loaned, given, traded, and, occasionally, fought over. Their intrinsic value was seldom, if ever, an issue. Furniture, silver, glass, china tended to be labeled not with their value, but by their previous owner. I had, for example, at home "Cousin Kate's desk," and "Cousin Julie's bookcase." The fact that the first dated from before the American Revolution and that the second was from the 1830s was less relevant. Generally speaking, the only time that money was associated with them was at a "family auction."

When one occurred, the belongings of some deceased member of the family would be sold at a private auction, one restricted to family members only. Competitive bidding arose when several members of the family wanted the same thing, not for its intrinsic value, but for the association they had with it. At this point, bidding could be not only spirited, but bitter, something the auctioneers played on to increase prices for the estate.

Family members did not frequent antique stores, or for that matter, go to department stores for home furnishings, even as wedding presents. We didn't have to. Like the ladies in Boston who "had their hats," we *had* our furniture.

Only once had the matter of real commercialism raised its head. My great-uncle Heyward had once gone to my great-uncle DeBruce and asked for a fine breakfront bookcase that used to occupy an upstairs hall in their parents' home. Uncle DeBruce, being an easygoing man, gave it to him. Uncle Heyward turned around and sold it to Colonial Williamsburg for $10,000. Ten thousand 1935 dollars, that is. It stands there today in the Governor's Palace. I located it once when I was there on a visit.

Uncle DeBruce was philosophical about it, if somewhat put out. "Hell," he was reported as saying, "If Heyward wanted to sell it he should have told me. *I* wouldn't have cared. It was just taking up houseroom. And besides, I never liked it very much anyway. Why didn't he play fair with me?"

The rest of the family was furious and never really trusted

Uncle Heyward again. At issue was family loyalty. The family knew that Uncle Heyward was a fool about money and had wasted his inheritance. It wasn't the money that got under their skin. He had been disloyal to his brother.

Even that episode did not make us think of family belongings as merchandise, as something that one might find in an antique store. If we had thought about it, we probably would have thought it ever-so-slightly beneath us.

As I thought this through, I realized that Wainwright was continuing to talk.

"I don't know enough about what you have here. Besides, I don't have the right contacts. Wish I could, though. You have a fortune in that house." He gestured toward the tumbledown front porch with its rickety stairs and sagging roof. "Tell you what I'll do, however, Let's go through some of the 'trash' on the porch so that you can see the kind of thing I have in mind."

We worked for the rest of the day. By its end, the three of us had segregated out a motley collection of fan boxes ("Put these back with those fans."), old hat and clothing boxes, old glass preserving jars ("The green ones are in great demand."), eight green glass telephone line insulators ("I charge eight dollars apiece for them in the City."), all of the cotton lisle stockings ("Some antique dealer will snap them up and sell them for Christmas stockings.") and a number of other things as well, including the cologne bottles ("Soak the tops in alcohol. That should loosen them.").

When Wainwright and Allen left, they refused to take anything with them except a few of Cousin Margaret's rose geranium plants from the hothouse. "I love these. My grandmother used to raise them," Wainwright said in parting.

After watching their car disappear down the driveway, I walked back into the house to do the locking up. They had stayed until sundown, and the evening shadows hung heavy upon the rooms as I walked through turning out lights and shutting windows. I had brought over a small portable radio I had purchased so I could listen to the news, and I turned it on in a lighted upstairs bedroom window that opened off the main entrance hall and was visible from the driveway. I had decided to ask my cousins Monday if they would let me stay in Cousin Margaret's apartment for safety, but I thought that the lights and a radio playing in the house would give a little protection in the meantime.

As I walked down the stairs, looking at the light pouring out of the open bedroom door, the nameless fear assailed me that there was someone in that upstairs bedroom. There was no reason for it, no possibility that there was anyone there. But, standing in the darkened hall with the hanging strips of torn wallpaper making strange patterns on the walls and every other open door a blank void, the feeling attacked the pit of my stomach with relentless intensity.

Seeking reassurance, I climbed the stairs to check again. Naturally, no one was there. The dim bulb illuminated the room's contents—broken chairs, a stack of barrels, wooden chests and trunks—but no being, human or otherwise, was to be seen. I turned my back on the strident music from the radio and walked back around the gallery.

I had just reached the top of the stairs when I heard footsteps and saw a light appearing from the kitchen. Terror-stricken, I let out a yelp and whirled to snap the nearest light switch. The hall chandelier sprang into light just as a figure holding a lighted flashlight came through the door from the dining room.

"Did I startle you? I'm sorry."

"You sure did. The house gives me the creeps at this time of day. Who are you?"

"I'm sorry. I should have introduced myself several days ago. I'm Frank Micciche, Miss Leverich's tenant."

He held out his hand, and I walked down to shake it. Frank was lean and craggy, bald, with glasses and a mustache. He had a pleasant smile.

"I remember," I said, "Cousin Margaret used to talk about you and your wife when she visited me on the West Coast. I'm her cousin, Russell Hunter. I've been meaning to come down and say hello, but somehow I got swallowed up here."

Frank looked around and smiled. "Not surprising. There is a lot here. It's a big house." He stopped for a few seconds and then went on. "Would you like to come down for a cup of coffee with us? My wife, Marian, would like to meet you. As a matter of fact, it was she who sent me up."

"I'd like that," I said. "Just a minute till I go back up and turn the light off."

"Won't have to." He walked over to a wall switch by the door leading to the living room hall. "The lights can be turned on or off from both this switch and the one at the top of the stairs."

He snapped the switch and the lights went out, leaving us in darkness. "Strange," I thought to myself. "He appears to know the house well." Something didn't fit. How did he know *that* much when Cousin Margaret had refused to allow both Lloyd and me to enter the house in years past?

I said nothing, however, and presently forgot the thought. Frank lighted us both out through the dark kitchen and servants' quarters with his flashlight. I locked the door behind us, and we both walked out into the warm June night. The smell of honeysuckle hung heavy in the air, reminding me pleasantly of years past both at Open Country and at Lacey Green. The world seemed more sane again.

We were walking down the driveway toward Frank's house, which used to be occupied by the head gardener and his family, when I noticed an irregular shadow, about a story high, standing out against the evening sky. Frank caught me looking at it.

"Do you know what that is?" he asked.

"Sure do. The Newtown House. It was moved up from Newtown, Long Island just after they bought this place. My cousins could never decide where to put it up, so they left it there to rot. I used to come down here and poke around in it when I was a child.

The house was quite old, I believe. There are about half a dozen mantelpieces from the house in the attic of the Big House."

"You know more about it than I do. All I know is that it is an eyesore. Miss Leverich was never willing to do anything about it," he added.

"What shape is it in?"

"Pretty bad. All dried out and rotten."

So much for that. Whatever the Newtown House had been, it was now just a pile of rotting lumber. Nothing, however, for us to worry about. Together, we walked to their house, where I was greeted warmly by Marian Micciche, a chubby woman with a motherly manner.

"We're so glad you got here. Miss Margaret was very fond of you. After each of her visits, she used to come down and tell us all about her visits to Los Angeles." She laughed. "She would talk about it for days after she got back. I don't think there was a minute of her visit that she didn't cover."

I wondered what they had thought about it. Had she told them all about what the men wore in Palm Springs and what the women didn't? And what had this pleasant country couple thought of her descriptions of the desert, of the ocean, of the plants in the hothouse whose cuttings I had sent back with her?

"I'm glad she enjoyed herself. She was a lot of fun."

"We're glad you're here for another reason too," Marian went on. "Did you know that the Big House has been entered once or twice?"

My interest was immediately aroused. "Well, my cousins wrote me that there had been a couple of attempts after she died. Once, apparently, someone got in, but didn't take anything. The second time, someone stole some of the rain gutters."

"Yes," Frank said, "they are all made of copper, and scrap copper brings a pretty good price these days."

How much, I wondered, had Rubino gotten for that roll of copper wire?

"The place was also robbed," Marian said, "before Miss Leverich died. She was very upset about it because they took a lot of valuable Wedgwood china. I remember seeing it in the china closet in the butler's pantry. She told me later that the insurance company gave her about two thousand dollars for it."

"That I didn't know about. But I'm glad it was insured."

"That's why I am so glad you are here," Marian said. We're so afraid that something else could happen. Frank noticed lights in the house one evening—it was before the leaves came out in the trees and we could still see the Big House—and went up to investigate."

"I didn't see where they got in," Frank said, "but they had left the lights on in the dining room. I called the police, and we looked around, but nothing seemed to have been disturbed. I guess maybe they heard me coming and ran away."

"Who knows where they got in," I said. "Breaking into that house is a cinch." I then told me of my break-and-entry when I first arrived.

"That's why we're so glad you got here," Marian said again, "We can't see the house now because of the leaves on the trees. Miss Leverich set great store by her things, and I'd hate to see anything happen. Would you like to stay with us?"

"That's very kind of you, but it might be better if I lived over the garage where she lived. At least I am close to the house there. I might even consider sleeping in the house at night. Then I would hear anyone coming in."

Frank frowned. "How would you get out if there was trouble? You'd scare a thief away, but we have a lot of trouble with vandals coming up from South Norwalk. If it was a bunch of kids out for trouble, you couldn't handle them."

"I know that house pretty well. If I slept in Miss Leverich's bedroom I could always escape through the servants' wing or down the back stairs, which lead to the hall off the living room. Do you know the one I mean?"

Frank looked thoughtful. "Yes, it leads down past that big old mirror that Miss Leverich thought so highly of. You'd have to go out by the kitchen or the living room, though. The door at the bottom of those stairs is stuck tight with damp."

"Well, it's an idea," I said.

Shortly afterward, I left and drove out of the driveway past the lighted windows of the Big House on my way to Tom and Dorli's.

Monday, when my cousins arrived from their weekend at home, I told them of Janet's visit and of Jordy's opinions, of Wainwright's visit, and of my gathering fears of the danger of theft or vandalism.

My cousins agreed that it would be a good idea to have me act as watchdog and also agreed to let me install a phone in Cousin Margaret's apartment. At their suggestion, I walked over to the Micciches' and called Janet to ask her over so that we could start unpacking dresses. I also arranged to have a phone installed.

I had just returned from this errand when I saw a jeep turning into the driveway. It was bright red, enclosed with canvas side curtains and convertible top, and was adorned with an enormous bright yellow snowplow in front that looked thoroughly out of place. The jeep drew up on the lawn, and Jordy got out.

"I thought I'd come over to meet your cousins and have another look," he said. "Janet will be along in a little while. She is taking Maria over to a friend's house."

I introduced him to my cousins, and we all walked over to the Big House. I led the way up the disappearing pull-down staircase to the attic to show my cousins the trunks and the six wooden mantels standing in the shadows.

"I say, old man," Lloyd said, "this is the first time we have been up here. There was so much work down below that the three of us didn't have the heart to look for more work. Have you any more surprises for us?"

"As a matter of fact, yes. Have you been in the cellar? There is a whole stack of marble down there. Probably two or three marble mantelpieces in pieces. The mantels here must have come from the Newtown House.

"One thing at a time, please. We were afraid of rats in the cellar and never went there. But what is the Newtown House?"

Briefly, I outlined its history and explained its probable condition. Then Katherine spoke up.

"I've counted ten trunks up here. Are there any others in the house?"

"Yes," I said. "There is one in the front bedroom and more in the sewing room off Cousin Margaret's bedroom."

Louise had opened one of the trunks and folded back some of the tissue wrappings, exposing the brilliant silks and velvets underneath. She turned from this display and cast a glance around the attic.

"We can't unpack these here. This attic is filthy, and it's too hot to work here."

"Why don't we carry the trunks downstairs?" Jordy said. "I'll help."

"Thanks," I said, "but do you really have the time?"

"I have loads of time. I'm going to Columbia for my MA in business administration in the fall, and I decided to take the summer off beforehand."

"Well," Lloyd said, "we certainly could use it. I'm not as young as I once was and"—looking at the trunks with some distaste—"those things look heavy."

"We've cleared Cousin Margaret's bedroom," Katherine said. "Why don't we take the trunks down there?"

By the time Janet arrived, all ten trunks were in the sewing room, and Lloyd, Jordy, and I were soaking with perspiration. Louise dragged a bolt of unbleached muslin out of the linen closet and spread it on the floor, and the three women set to work unpacking the dresses.

"How are we ever going to store all these?" Louise asked when one tray had been unpacked and its contents laid out on the clean muslin. A brilliant, canary-colored watered-silk evening dress with a hoop skirt containing yards of material and a white satin wedding dress of the same era, trimmed generously with handmade lace, seemed to fill up half the room.

"If we can find enough wire hangers in the house and the apartment, "Katherine said, "we can hang them in the closets we cleared on Friday."

Janet spoke up. "If you'd like, I can arrange the dresses chronologically just as we do at the museum. We can call one closet 1850–1870, one 1870–1890 and so on."

"Fine," said Louise. "Katherine and I will unpack the dresses and put them on hangers, and you can arrange them for us. That way, we will have some idea of what we have when we are all through."

Leaving the three women deep in piles of tissue paper and silks, Jordy and I walked back to the bow-front bureau he had remarked on the night before.

"Can you tell me something about this, Jordy?" I asked. "What makes it valuable? It is nice piece of furniture—the satinwood has a magnificent sheen—but what makes it worth three hundred dollars?"

"I said I might be willing to pay three hundred dollars for it if the brasses were original," he replied. "Actually, you might be able to get more for it, but that is as high as I would go. This piece was made in the United States, probably around 1800. We call that the Federal Period. Collectors will pay high prices for furniture from that period and earlier if"—and he put emphasis on the word *if*—"the furniture has not been altered in any way."

"What do you mean 'altered'?" I asked.

"A lot of times with very old pieces, some later owner will want the piece lowered and have a portion of the legs taken off. Sometimes also an attempt was made to 'update' a piece by putting new brass handles on drawers and doors. A lot of this was done during the Victorian era when machine-tooling made it possible to produce fancier brasses than was possible with the old hand methods."

Jordy pulled out one of the drawers and looked underneath it. "I can tell this is a genuine Federal piece and not a copy because of the hand-fitted bottoms to the drawers. Also, the wood was cut with a hand saw. You can see the straight saw marks. The rotary saw, which came later, leaves rounded saw marks. These brasses look original to me."

He looked at the back of the front panel of the drawer. "You see, these are the original holes. In most cases when new handles were put in, new holes were drilled because the new handles did not match the old holes.

"I'll stick with my original three-hundred-dollar offer," Jordy continued. "Keep it in mind. You might be able to do better somewhere else, but if a dealer offers you less, I'll still pay the three hundred."

We were interrupted by the arrival of the telephone man to install the phones. After I had shown him were they were to go, Jordy and I continued to walk through the house, inspecting the furniture. Jordy upended chairs to look at the corner bracing, removed drawers, peered behind cabinets, inspected studded brass fittings and inlaid wood, all the while keeping up a running commentary on what he saw. By the end of our tour, I had learned a great deal about how one went about judging old furniture. Finally, he faced me directly.

"Russell," he said, "you have a lot of Empire and Victorian furniture that isn't very valuable. You also have a few nice pieces. There is nothing of outstanding value here, nor real collectors' 'finds' but you *do* have some very nice furniture. Be very careful how you sell them. Don't sell through one antique dealer. Have a number of them come through. You'll learn a lot that way, far more than I can tell you."

Together, we walked back to Cousin Margaret's bedroom, which looked startlingly like a dressmaker's shop from a bygone era. An enormous pile of tissue paper almost blocked the entrance, and inside the room there was an impenetrable tangle of silks and velvets, chiffon and lace, hats of all kinds, and tiny, tiny satin slippers.

Janet looked up from her work with a smile as we came in. "Things are not as bad as they look. Everything was carefully labeled, but not all the dresses are complete." She held up a bodice of emerald silk trimmed with white lace. "See this? We can't find the skirt to it anywhere. We know who wore it, but someone must have taken the skirt that belonged to it and remodeled it, leaving only this." She put it down with a worried frown. "Still, you have some magnificent dresses here, and Miss Miller at the Museum will be thrilled to see them. There are three real finds. Here," she said, leading me over to an open closet.

Inside the closet, hanging on a wire hanger, was a filmy cotton dress rather like a nightgown but with a short train. Beside it hung a tan silk brocade dress and a white silk dress covered with flowers delicately embroidered in many colors.

"These really are superb. The two silk dresses are definitely eighteenth century and very rare. We repaired one for Winterhalter, the DuPont museum. They bought it for a handsome sum, I know, and it wasn't in nearly as good condition as this is. And this"—indicating the cotton dress—"is a cotton piqué Empire gown."

"Empire? What empire? Sorry, but it looks like an old nightgown to me."

Janet smiled. "Too long since you studied history, Russell. Napoleon's empire." She touched the material again, "These are very rare indeed. People didn't hold onto cotton the way they did the finer materials, and any museum would be delighted to get this.

A mischievous smile came to Janet's face. "An old nightgown? You may have a point there. This style of dress was Napoleon's idea. He wanted to increase the birth rate in France, and he made the women give up the stiff and binding corsets they had been accustomed to wearing for years and substituted the high-waisted style we call Empire, one that required fewer undergarments.

"Some of the ladies used to dampen the light petticoats they wore under these dresses so they would cling to their legs and make them more attractive. It was a racy age, and, when this style went out of fashion, men had to wait a hundred years before they could tell what a woman really looked like when she walked down the street."

Serious, she turned to the other dresses in the room. "Many of these dresses date from before the Civil War, and I know Miss Miller will hope you will donate them to the museum. The others, especially those from the eighties and nineties, I'm not so sure about. You may have trouble disposing of those."

"Could you get in touch with her for us if we do decide we want to give them away? You know and understand what is here and she might be more willing to come and see for herself if she had word from an expert," I said.

"I'd love to. I haven't seen her since I left the Museum to get married, and maybe she could come up for a weekend. It'll take more than one day to pack all the dresses I know she'll want."

Louise spoke up. "Russell, did you know we also found a lot of dolls? Janet says they may be quite valuable. Here, take a look.," she said, opening the double doors of a closet.

I looked in. It was full of miniature furniture, perfect in every detail. One bedroom set was carved entirely from ivory. There was a dining room set with a table and sideboard topped with real marble. A little cast-iron stove sat on one shelf, surrounded by cooking utensils. Opening the firebox, I found that it burned coal and had been used many times to boil water for dolls' tea or to make miniature stews for doll consumption.

There were tea sets and dinner sets, complete with realistic make-believe food on the plates. A cigar box held a variety of tiny bric-a-brac items in miniature, little candelabras, pitchers, bowls, vases of flowers—each perfect in every detail. From one shelf, a doll with a silk and velvet bustled dress from the eighties gazed out at me; beside her lay three others costumed in the same style, complete with hats, shoes, and lace-edged undergarments.

One doll stood upright, a jaunty cap on her head and a starched crinoline spread generously around her. I picked her up and found that the crinoline concealed a little clockwork motor and tiny tricycle. When I wound her up, she ran in a little circle, shaking her head from side to side as she moved. Under what candlelit Christmas tree had she first sat, I wondered?

There was also a doll dressed in gingham and a poke bonnet, carrying a tray full of miniature mirrors, scissors, rolls of ribbon, and all manner of miniature sewing equipment. Was she a model, I wondered, of the peddler women who plied their trade on the streets of New York, selling such things to passersby before the days of the five and dime (itself now a thing of the past)?

Janet joined me. "These are quite valuable. Miss Miller would kill me for saying this, for the Museum would love to have them, but you can sell these to collectors. I don't know much about dolls, so I can't give you any idea of what each one is worth, but I know these can be sold. The Peddler Doll is quite old. I know that from her costume. And I believe that clockwork dolls are also quite rare." Together, we shut the door on the closet containing the dolls.

"I'll be back tomorrow," Janet said. "To finish the work of arranging and cataloging the dresses. I think we have enough closets so that we can hang them all up properly behind closed doors so they won't get dusty. Then, later in the summer, we can get in touch with the Museum if you want."

After everyone had left the house, I made up my mind to start sleeping the in the Big House. Suddenly, surrounded by the rich display of silks and velvets from the past, increasingly aware of the value of the furniture and other things in the house, I began to dread the possibility of vandalism. It would be bad enough to have valuable things stolen, but the idea that this rich heritage from the past might be damaged by irresponsible people genuinely horrified me.

I could not bear the idea of leaving the house unprotected, and I decided to begin my guard duty at once. Taking sheets and blankets from the enormous supply in the linen closet, I made up the bed in Cousin Margaret's bedroom before returning to Tom and Dorli's for dinner.

Returning later from a relaxing dinner, I felt a chill steal over me as the headlights fell upon the bleak outlines of the house. There was a full moon, and the unpainted shingles, battered shutters, and sagging porches stood out in ghostly detail. Walking through the house did not improve the state of my nerves any more than my previous nighttime visits had.

Settling down in bed surrounded by the rich tangle of silk and velvet, I turned out the light, only to find that the wisteria vines, which had grown through the windows from the lattice outside and looked cheerful and green during the day, assumed a menacing aspect against the bright moonlight outside.

Determinedly, I shut my eyes and relaxed for sleep. Lying the darkness, I learned at once that the house was not as silent as I had thought. Minute mutterings and flutterings filled the house, chasing chills up and down my spine. The great hall several rooms away magnified those sounds like some giant echo chamber and channeled them through the door behind me.

As I drifted into uneasy sleep, the sound of scrabbling in the attic above brought me back to instant wakefulness. My eyes snapped open and my body stiffened before I realized I must be listening to chipmunks or mice chasing around the bare attic floor. "Only that and nothing more," I said to myself.

Uneasily, I once more closed my eyes and tried to sleep. Still, the eerie symphony of sounds invaded my consciousness. The sound of leaves moving gently in the wind, the odd creakings of any old house at night, a branch brushing the side of the house—all conspired with my imagination to keep my body stiff, my eyes wide open.

Picking up the flashlight from the table beside me, I scrambled out of bed and made my way barefoot through the house, looking for I knew not what, turning on the lights as I went. Room after room looked the same as when the house had been inhabited during the day. The bare globes showed the same cracked and crumbled plaster, the same bare floors, the same furniture standing mute against the walls. I made a complete tour of the house, finding nothing, and finally forced myself to return to bed, turning off lights as I went.

Once more, I lay down and forced my eyes closed. The sounds of the house were more familiar now, more identifiable, and easier to sleep with. I was just drifting off again when a single sound, a thump, came resounding up to me from the great hall. Rigid with fear, I lay listening, trying to figure out what this new sound might be. No second thump came, and I relaxed gradually to sleep once more.

Suddenly, it came again; that single thump throbbing through the empty rooms, sending an echo of chills down my spine. I raised on one elbow and listened, straining for some other sound that might tell me what it was, but there was none. No footfall, not sound of breathing. Nothing.

Without warning, it came again out of the darkness of the rooms behind me, that nameless thump. Unreasoning, I flung myself out of bed and, without stopping to pick up my flashlight, wrapped my sheet and blankets around me, hurried through the shadowy rooms and down the stairs, past the two lighted bedrooms in the front of the house, past the great shadow of the kitchen range, and out the servants' quarters. When my feet hit the chill dew on the grass outside, I heaved a great sigh of relief and trailed my bedding across the lawn to the garage and the safety of Cousin Margaret's apartment. I flung myself down on her couch, gradually relaxed, and drifted off to a deep sleep.

"Good morning! Early riser aren't you?" I opened my eyes to see Lloyd standing in the middle of the living room, looking at me amusedly through his spectacles. Louise was in the kitchen making coffee. The sun was pouring through the windows, and, as I unwrapped my bedding I got up, feeling very foolish, rather like a man who, the Morning After, remembers exactly what he did the night before.

I looked at my watch. "Heavens, it's ten o'clock!"

"Nothing wrong with sleeping late, old man," Lloyd said. "Could do with a bit of it myself. Big night last night?" Again the eyes twinkled understandingly. "Could do with a bit of that too from time to time."

"Wish it had been. No, it was a big night of a different kind. Tried to sleep in the Big House last night. I decided after you two left that there were just too many valuable things lying around to be left alone. Had dinner at Tom and Dorli's and then returned, intending to spend the night in Cousin Margaret's bedroom."

"What made you leave? Ghosts?"

Shamefacedly, I repeated to him my fears during the night before. I was interrupted by the sound of a car outside and a cheerful shout. Looking out, I saw that Bennet and Jordy had just driven in. Jordy was driving the jeep, minus its snowplow, and Bennet had their station wagon. They opened the door of the apartment before I managed to put away my tangle of bedclothes.

"Great heavens, Russell," Bennet said. "Couldn't you make it to the bedroom last night? Just what did you have to drink at Tom and Dorli's? And how much?"

Once again, I repeated my sad tale of the night before. It sounded more foolish every time I told it. When Jordy and Bennet had finished laughing, Bennet spoke up.

"I thought I'd come over and help with the dresses and take a look at some of the furniture Jordy has been talking about. We brought over the jeep because we thought you might need it. You said the other day that you were thinking of buying a truck. Why don't you borrow the jeep in the meantime? You can use the back to haul trash. Jordy says you have a lot of it."

"An enormous amount. But won't you need it?"

"No. We only use it in winter when we have to plow out the

drive. It has four-wheel drive so it won't get stuck, and you could use it to drag the trash out to the garden to burn.

"Well," I said, "we sure could use it, and I would like to take Vic and Lenee's car back to them. Lenee is stranded at home during the day without it. Have you any idea where I might pick up a truck?"

"Tator's Garage," Jordy said. "It's only about three miles from here. I'll take you down today. Maybe they'll know someone who has one for sale."

"Fine."

A few minutes later, Janet drove in. After she, too, had been regaled with my tale of my midnight flight, we all returned to work in the Big House.

Bennet was pop-eyed at the display of dresses and cheerfully threw herself into the work of unpacking and sorting dresses. Jordy, Lloyd, and I busied ourselves with taking the accumulated trash out to the front porch.

"Going to try and sleep here again?" Jordy asked.

"I don't think I've got the guts. I'm still worried about vandalism, and I do plan to move into Cousin Margaret's apartment, but I can't face another night here alone. Wish I could, but I can't."

"Why don't you have the house posted?" Jordy asked.

"What's that?"

"A lot of people who come up here only for the summer do it. When they leave in the fall, the State Police post a sign on the property saying the place is under their protection, and they patrol it regularly. That helps keep sneak thieves away. I don't know if they do it during the summer, but you could ask them."

"I'll do it right now." I went to the telephone and called the nearest State Police barracks. The sergeant promised to send someone around, and that afternoon, two troopers showed up and introduced themselves as John Tengstrom and Bob Duffel.

"I know this place rather well," Tengstrom said. "Miss Leverich had a robbery here last fall, and I came over to see her about it. I didn't get to see the inside of the house, but I sure was curious."

"My cousin was sensitive about showing people through," I replied. "Perhaps you had better go through it with me so we can see what our problem is."

As we walked through the house, I pointed out the values of the things I knew about. When we reached Cousin Margaret's, bedroom, I found that the job of cataloging dresses was almost complete. The dresses filled a total of eight closets in her bedroom and the adjoining bedroom.

The eighteenth century and Empire dresses were in one closet. Those from the 1850s and 1860s were in another closet; those from the 1870s took up two closets; those from the 1880s and 1890s took two more; and the rest were in the remaining two closets. There were a few dresses from the 1900–1910 period and a few from the next decade, but nothing from the 1920s except for Cousin Jessie's one evening dress. Janet explained the value of the dresses to the two men.

"You have an enormous collection here," Tengstrom said when she was through. "I know someone nearby who would like to see what you have. He is the curator of the John Jay museum in Katonah. They are restoring John Jay's house down there, and I know he'd like to see your things. He is always interested in antiques."

Bennet spoke up. "That's Lewis Rubinstein, isn't it? John Jay is an ancestor of mine, and he went to Mother's a number of times trying to persuade her to donate some of John Jay's things."

"Yes," said Tengstrom, "it's Rubenstein." He turned to me. "May I bring him by? I get off work in a couple of hours, and we might come by this afternoon."

"By all means. I'd be happy to see him through."

"To get back to your problem," Tengstrom went on, "you do have a problem here. Is anybody living on the property?"

"Yes," I replied, "I am living in Miss Leverich's apartment over the garage. And beside me, Miss Leverich's tenants, Mr. and Mrs. Micciche, live at the back of the property."

"Frank Micciche?"

"Yes. Do you know him?"

"Yes, indeed. He is a volunteer fireman," Tengstrom said. "It's a little easier if there is someone living here. I'll tell you what I think we can do. We don't usually post houses except during the winter, but there are some posters left over from last winter at the barracks, and I can give you a couple or three to put about the house.

"Put them in the windows where they can be seen from outside. That'll help keep people away. In addition, leave some lights on and leave your radio playing inside the house. I'll ask the sergeant if we can have a patrol car swing through here once a night."

"Boy," I said. "That'll be a help. I tried to sleep in the house last night, but I couldn't face it. I probably couldn't hear anyone in the house from Miss Leverich's apartment, but I would feel much more comfortable knowing you boys are coming by once a night."

"I'll ask the sergeant," Tengstrom said. "We'd better be going. I'll try to bring Rubinstein back this afternoon, and I'll bring the posters back with me then."

He and Duffle got back into their patrol car and drove away. About three hours later, he was back with the posters. He told us where to put them and then said that Rubinstein was out of town for a few days and that he would bring him over when he returned. After they left, I placed the placards they had given me in ground-floor windows around the house, where they gave me comfort for the balance of the summer.

It rained during the night, and when I arose the next morning, I suggested that we make a start toward getting rid of the trash on the front porch and in the servants' quarters, which had filled both places to overflowing.

Mindful of what John Wainwright had told me, I first sorted through the material on the front porch that he had identified as salable and then settled down to the task of getting the real trash out to the vegetable garden.

Presently, as he was to do almost daily when there was work to do, Jordy appeared and set to work with us, dragging the leftover trash out to the vegetable garden. As time went by, we came to call it the Burning Ghat, after those areas that the Hindus in India used to immolate their dead.

Jordy and I concentrated upon the lugging, while Lloyd stood by the fires with the Indian pump Katherine had brought the day before in case the fire should get out of hand. It did us good to dispose of these leavings. In the first place, they cluttered up areas where we badly needed space to work, and in the second place, the trash was a depressing reminder of the sad nature of our work.

We seemed to be writing finis to half-a-dozen areas at one time. The relics of the immediate past, bundle after bundle of crossword puzzles, hoarded matchboxes, candy boxes, and Bab-O containers mingled in the flames with Italian straw basket souvenirs from the nineties too tattered for sale.

The variety was enormous—spectacles belonging to cousins already dead when I was born, writing paper from past family residences, faded and rotted silk scarves and veils from the early 1900s, packets of fine kid gloves, hairpins and combs long since gone out of style, ancient broad-brimmed straw hats trimmed with ribbons and flowers faded with age, and countless small, battered little boxes that had contained everything from jewelry to pills.

The list seemed to go on forever: formal engraved calling cards bearing the names of Cousin Margaret's mother, of her sister, of herself; seed and feed catalogs from the days when my cousins were "gentleman farmers." These were burned alongside hoarded rolls from toilet tissue ("To roll odd pieces of used ribbon on").

We all felt tired but enormously relieved in spirit when this depressing hoard of trash had at long last disappeared into the flames and been reduced to ashes. We all knew that much more of the same lay hidden in the chests and closets in the Big House and in Cousin Margaret's little apartment, but the porch and the servants' wing were clear, and we felt as if a huge load had been lifted from our hearts.

When we returned to the Big House after watching the last

of the flames die down, we found that Katherine and Louise had unearthed additional finery—and additional problems as well. Cousin Margaret's wing was completely unpacked, and Katherine and Louise eagerly showed us the results of their work.

Two closets and a wardrobe were completely full of a rich variety of curtains. The shelves glowed with rich colors—brilliant brocaded silks, cut velvet and plush, fancy curtain tiebacks made of silken tasseled ropes. There was also a bell-pull made of blue and white glass beads and a box full of baroque gilt curtain tiebacks. More modest, but in greater profusion, were Victorian lace curtains, a variety of printed cotton and linen curtains, and a huge number of ruffled cambric curtains.

"These," said Louise, "are our real finds." She led the way to a third closet. "I wish Janet were still here, for she would know a lot more about these than I do, but I know they are very old and quite good."

She opened up an enormous patchwork quilt, its intricate design and bright colors unfaded."This one was never finished," Louise went on. "According to this note, it was made by Cousin Margaret's great-aunt Caroline. It should have been quilted like the rest of these"—gesturing at the other shelves—"but she evidently never finished it. All the rest are, I think, much older. They are a little faded, but the workmanship is magnificent."

"The most beautiful thing here," Katherine said, "unfortunately isn't ours. Feast your eyes on this."

Dramatically, she flipped opened an apparently plain green silk quilted comforter. The reverse side was a symphony of rich color, a geometric design worked out entirely in silks in many colors. There was a note attached in Cousin Margaret's handwriting. "Made by Mrs. Bowen, our old nurse, when I was a child and given to Mrs. Raymond Martin. The white squares came from Aunt Mim's wedding dress. Mrs. Martin loaned it back to me on the understanding that I would leave it to her granddaughter, Laura, when I died, MDL."

"Isn't it a shame," Katherine said. "It's magnificent. Still, we can't really go back on Cousin Margaret's request, can we?"

"Now that you've had your fun," Katherine went on, "come and look at our problem." Katherine led the way to the next room, where I saw a stack of cardboard boxes, apparently full of papers. "Here," she said, picking up a card from the top box. "Since this concerns you, you might begin by looking at this."

I took it from her and read, "The Misses Leverich cordially invite you to a small tea in honor of Miss Martha M. Russell on April 23, 1923." My mother. A relic of the ordeal of family inspection undergone when she and my father became engaged.

"Great God," I said. "Didn't they throw anything out?"

"A most interesting family," Katherine replied with a sour smile. "The rest of these boxes are full of letters, checkbooks, and all manner of other records. We opened one or two and this is what we found."

She held out an envelope for me to open. Inside, I found a letter from a lawyer in Louisiana and three checks for $478.95, written out to Cousin Henry, Cousin Margaret, and Cousin Catherine. All were dated October 19, 1923.

"They were so damn rich in those days they didn't even bother to cash their checks. I'll be she could have used these in the thirties. For that matter, I could use them right now. Do you suppose they are still good?"

"I doubt it," I replied. "But we can ask Mr. Quinn about this."

"In the meantime," Louise said, "what do we do with all this stuff? We have found a couple of dollar bills in these letters and other uncashed checks as well. Some of them are dated before World War I, and they were apparently written to Cousin Margaret when she was treasurer of some civic organization, the Women's Athletic League. We can't throw out the letters because there might be more money there; and besides, the stamps might be valuable. But it would take a long time to go through them."

"There are other cases of letters elsewhere about the house," I said. "Perhaps we had better find a place to put them and collect them all in one room."

"Where can we put them?" Katherine asked.

"Well," I said, "there is a little cubbyhole, about six by six, just off the living room. It's not much good for anything else. Why don't we make that the Family Paper Room? We can accumulate all the papers there. As a matter of fact, it already has some boxes of papers in it, I think. Seem to be records of an old company. The boxes were marked "Leverich and Co." and a lot of dates, mostly in the seventies. Heaven knows what we will do with them, but we might as well put them in one place."

"Sounds all right with me," Katherine said, turning to Lloyd. "What do you think?"

"Fine with me, old girl," Lloyd said. "But not today. I've done all the carrying I want to do for one day."

"Amen," Katherine replied. "Just one more thing. That trunk over there," she said, gesturing toward a great Saratoga trunk, "seems to be full of furs."

"Furs?" I said. "What kind of furs?"

"Some bear rugs, something that looks like caribou hide and some sheepskins with the fleece still on them. And those packages over there seem to contain rugs."

"Let's just leave them packed away until later," I replied. "We know what they are, and they'll only take up space if we unpack them."

Katherine sighed. "Let's go back to the apartment for a drink. I'm exhausted. But at least we have finished this wing. The living room below shouldn't be so hard. No closets." Together, we locked up the house and returned to the cozy atmosphere of Cousin Margaret's apartment.

Chapter 6

This Is a Rare Experience We're Having

The next day, Katherine and I were alone in the house. My cousins had finished clearing Cousin Margaret's wing the day before, and Katherine and I walked about the house looking for someplace to make a new start.

"You know," Katherine said, "there is one room I've been itching to get at."

"Which one?"

"You know the bedroom off the main hall, the second-floor one with all the barrels in it?"

"Yes, indeed. That's one of the two I keep lit at night."

"Why don't we attack that? I'm dying to see what's in those barrels."

"Fine with me."

Together, we started to work. I began by carrying out a number of broken chairs and tables that were stored there.

"I think I'll take these down to the living room. There are a lot of little chairs and tables there already, and we might make that the place we keep small pieces of furniture. I'll also take this wardrobe and the bookcase outside so we have room to work." I said. Katherine nodded, intent on opening the first barrel.

When I returned to the room, Katherine was standing by the window looking at a small cup in her hand.

"Russell, will you look at this? It is one of the most exquisite things I've ever seen."

I picked it up. As I did so, I remembered I had looked at it previously during my initial solitary walk through the house, but I had been so bemused by what I had already seen in the house that I had paid it little attention. The cup was light as a feather. The china was so thin that an eggshell might seem almost coarse by comparison, and it was so transparent that you could have almost read through it. The china was white and covered with intricate oriental scenes and animals in finely detailed gold and red. There were little people, dragons, and temples mingled in the profusion around the outside, and, in the oriental style, it lacked handles.

"It was the first thing I picked out, Russell," she said. "Why didn't she sell these things? I can understand why she didn't have the strength to deal with this other stuff"—gesturing at the tangle of broken furniture, old suitcases, dirt, and wicker baskets with which the room was crammed—"but why didn't she sell things like this and live better?"

The question was unanswerable. "I don't know. What I want to know now is how we can store this and the other things still in the barrels so that they don't get broken. What's in that closet?"

I opened the closet door and found that it was jammed full of fireplace equipment. Several fire screens were standing on the floor, and the shelves were jammed with wrought-iron and brass andirons. A fine wrought-iron hanging lantern took up additional floor space, and there was a box sitting on a high shelf. I took it down and found that it contained several locks that seemed to be designed to fit on the *outside* rather than the inside of a door, a number of obviously hand-wrought keys and half a dozen brass doorknobs. They did not match anything I had seen in the house thus far.

"Why don't I take all this fireplace stuff down to the fireplace in the hall? Then we can store the china in here. If we run out of space down in the dining room we can stack the wicker baskets against the windows. Then we will have a place to put them and people won't be able to look through the windows."

"I'd be grateful," Katherine said. "I can't take stairs as I used to or I'd help you. We certainly need the space in here. I'll unpack slowly so you can have some of the fun of discovery too."

"I don't like stairs either, but, thank heaven, I'll be carrying things down, not up."

Katherine sweetened each return trip I made by showing me some latest discovery as I walked back into the room. One of the first was a straight-sided cup with a deep saucer.

"Here," she said, "I think this may really belong to you"

"Why?"

"Look the label on the bottom."

I turned it over. Pasted to the bottom, in Cousin Margaret's hand, was a small piece of paper reading "Given to MDL by AMH, 1932."

"AMH was your uncle, wasn't he?" I asked.

"Yes. One of the suitcases I carried downstairs belonged to him. She must have agreed to store some of his things after my aunt Anne died and then forgotten them.

"I know this kind of thing quite well. It's Chinese export porcelain. I have seven of these on the West Coast. They're quite valuable. An antique dealer who came to my house offered me twenty-five dollars apiece for the cups and saucers."

"Why so much?"

"They are quite rare. There was a lively trade between New England and China in the 1760s in both porcelain and tea that I learned about when I went down to Washington and Williamsburg on my motorcycle some years ago (Katherine raised her eyebrows in surprise but made no comment). I learned a lot when I was down there.

"Clipper ships went around the Horn and brought back

what is now called 'Chinese export porcelain.' I saw a lot of it at Williamsburg. That's where I learned what it was and where it came from. Collectors pay good prices for pieces like this."

Katherine's other finds were equally spectacular. By the time I finished lugging the old iron and basketware out of the room, she had found fourteen of the Chinese export cups and saucers and ten of the eggshell porcelain cups she had first shown me, each with its little saucer. They were in perfect condition.

Together, we dragged the wardrobe and the bookcase in from the hall outside to contain our finds, and we continued our unpacking. Our finds covered an enormous spectrum. We found a tall Tiffany vase in the shape of a Jack-in-the-pulpit and a number of fine cut-crystal decanters.

We also found a dozen Meissen dessert plates and an enormous Sèvres compote on a gilt stand with two matching candy dishes, each bearing a crown and the initials LP.

Katherine examined the last finds with a puzzled look on her face. "LP? Doesn't look like a family piece. Do you know any family members with those initials?"

"No, but I know where this set of plates came from. The initials are those of Louis Phillipe, King of the French. Grandpa Schuchardt was in Paris during the Revolution of 1848 ..." Katherine again raised her eyebrows in astonishment.

"They went to Europe in 1848? During a revolution? An adventurous pair."

"No, Grandpa Schuchardt was probably alone. It would have been on his Grand Tour."

"What was that?"

"Young men from wealthy families were sometimes sent on a tour of Europe as an educational exercise. He would likely have gone to France, Italy, and perhaps Germany as well.

"Paris does not exactly sound like a safe place to be at the time, but Grandpa Schuchardt was outside the Tuileries Palace when a mob was sacking and burning the building, and he found a little boy with a stack of plates and other things beside him. The kid was smashing them on the cobblestones just for fun and Grandpa bought them for five francs. At least, that is the story behind half a dozen soup plates we used to have at home. He must have picked up these things at the same time. I now wonder if he paid the kid to steal some more stuff from the Tuileries. There is a lot more in the family than just a few dishes."

"They must be worth a mint" was Katherine's comment.

Near the bottom of the last barrel, I found three engraved crystal goblets and a small cut-crystal vase. The vase bore the date 1684 engraved as part of the design. The other two must have been almost as old; they bore rude engravings of figures dressed in the style of the mid-eighteenth century or earlier.

"What do you make of these?" Katherine asked.

"Dunno. I don't know much about glass. They look German, somehow. Grandpa Schuchardt may have picked them up when he was on his trip. The Schuchardts had come over in the early eighteenth century from Germany and he may have bought them as souvenirs."

"We'll never know." Katherine stopped speaking and gazed around her at our finds. She sat down on a small side chair I had not yet taken downstairs and shook her head.

"You know, Russell, this is a rare experience we're having. Sometimes I cannot really believe it myself," she said with a wave of her hand that included the brilliant colors of the china and stained glass on the shelves amid the cracked plaster and faded wallpaper around us.

"Once in a lifetime." She stopped. "No, only once in several lifetimes, would someone have the experience of finding treasures like this."

"Quite right. It almost overpowers you."

Momentarily, she seemed lost in thought and then she went on with a wave of her hand that took in all of the great hall outside and the other rooms in the house.

"Have you any idea how much time this has all taken?"

I frowned and shook my head. "What do you mean? All the unpacking we have to do?"

"No. All the time it took Cousin Margaret to sort and pack everything up. Everything she wrapped up and put away so carefully has a label written on it in her own handwriting. Not only did she want us to have all her stuff, she wanted us to know who owned it and when.

"She packed up all those rooms, all of those trunks and bureau drawers alone, with her own hands. She must have worked for hours. No, for weeks on end, if not months and maybe years. And now we are going to throw a lot of it out because it is worthless."

"A pity. But what else can we do?"

"Nothing. All we *can* do is to separate out the chaff and ensure that the valuable stuff is dealt with with the respect it deserves."

Suddenly aware of the amount of work my little cousin had done, I could only nod.

Together, we tossed the huge pile of packing materials and tissue paper off the balcony, where it seemed to almost fill the hall below, and I carried the empty barrels downstairs. It would not be long before the Burning Ghat would be in use again.

This was another example of Cousin Margaret simply storing things with little regard for their value. The barrels would likely have come up to Open Country forty or so years before, from Newtown, been stored haphazardly where the movers put them, and then been forgotten during the period when Cousin Margaret was eking out a living selling a few things to family with total disregard of other things of value in the house.

In a way, the house was beginning to shake down. One floor of the two wings was completely finished; the living room was becoming a repository of small furniture; the dining room for basketware, of which there was a good deal about the house; and the upstairs front bedroom seemed to have become the China Room.

Later that evening, Jordy phoned to tell me he had located a truck at Tator's Garage and suggested that he and I go down to look at it. It was, he said, a 1946 Dodge pickup formerly used on a big estate nearby. It had only twenty-four thousand original miles on it and had had an engine job just four thousand miles before. When I asked him why the mileage was so low, he explained that estate trucks like that one were rarely used off the estate and did not pile up mileage. He said that his source was honest, and, with that, I agreed to drive down with him.

The truck was not a pretty sight. The cab had once been dark blue but had oxidized to a mottled purple. One front fender had been replaced, but the replacement had never been painted so that its original gray rustproof paint stood out in all its dull splendor. The original body had been replaced with a dark green one whose fenders did not match the placement of the rear wheels. The deck was a mass of rust, and there was no tailgate.

Still, the $150 price tag took the sting out of the truck's appearance, the brakes had passed the New York State inspections, and the motor ran without audible clatter, so I accepted it as it was. Friends labeled it "The Perambulating Eyesore," shortened almost immediately to "The Eyesore." Later in the summer, it developed the habit of blowing the fuse that supplied the lights, and it was occasionally called the "Sightless Eyesore," when not called by richer and less printable names.

The following morning, when my cousins arrived, they wrinkled their noses at my purchase but agreed that, for the price, it was indeed a bargain. Katherine's eighteen-year-old son, Bill, had come up with her, and he immediately put in a bid for it when I no longer needed it, which to some extent restored my faith in my own judgment.

Bill was fascinated by the house. Like everyone else who was exposed to it, he became lost in the vastness of its rooms and the variety of its contents. In addition, like everyone else, he reacted in his own special way. An adventuresome spirit by nature, he decided that there must be a hidden room or closet somewhere, and spent much of the day grubbing about in the cellar and attics looking for space not accounted for in the rooms with which we were familiar.

Because the house had grown in so many directions and at so many times, it was a hodgepodge of little corners, blocked-up doors, and narrow little hallways. There was some basis for Bill's opinion, for there was at least one area of the house where the space between the walls of two rooms was six feet thick, which would have accounted for either a small room or a blocked-up stairway.

My two architect friends, Victor Koechel and Tom Bates, had found a similar space concealing a room in an eighteenth century house they were remodeling. The one that they found was entered through a loose board in the attic floor, and it was similar to the "priests' holes" in old English houses dating from the sixteenth century persecution of Roman Catholics.

Lacking another explanation, they decided that the room they found had played its part in the Underground Railway of pre–Civil War times and was part of the network of hiding places provided for runaway slaves on their way to Canada. Vic and Tom had explored the cellars earlier that summer and had told me that Open Country had originally been a Colonial building. Unlike Vic and Tom, however, we never found an entrance to the space between the walls.

Bill's search of the cellar, however, did turn up some fine cast-iron fireplace linings in varying patterns. One of them, a delicate sunburst design we later found dated to about 1810, was quite valuable. He had found it stacked in the crawl space beneath the living room, behind the furnace. Stacked with it were some hot-air vents of Victorian manufacture, an old hot water boiler, and some wicker furniture. No one could figure out why someone had taken the trouble to store them there because the space was cramped, being barely three feet high.

In the attic, Bill found a small box that had escaped our notice when we were dragging out the trunks of dresses. It was very heavy for its size and turned out to be full of little packages of stone wrapped in paper. On top, unwrapped, was an ancient carved marble head and a flat piece of marble covered with an inscription in Latin. More souvenirs of Grandpa Schuchardt's Grand Tour or of more recent vintage? There was no way of knowing, but there were family tales of him having bought "souvenirs" from workmen excavating the results of Vesuvius's eruption in Roman times.

When we came to unwrap the packages downstairs, we found that they contained small sample pieces of marble, each with an inscription showing the names of churches or *pallazi* carved in the face. There were several more pieces of ancient, inscribed marble and another piece of statuary broken off at the neck. We also found a little wooden box filled with curious little pieces of glass that were all twisted as if they had been in a fire. They were probably "souvenirs" of Pompeii as well and therefore quite possibly dated from the AD 79 Mt. Vesuvius eruption that leveled that Roman town.

I then remembered a pair of bronze gods that had stood on the mantelpiece at Open Country when I was a child, though I had not seen them on my first trip through the house, and they never appeared. Our finds could only have been collected in the days when families traveled with several trunks, a contrast to today when we are lucky to be able to put our traveling gear in a little compartment above our seats. The reader is encouraged to wonder whether the airplane really represents progress.

The real "buried treasure" of the summer turned up not as a result of deliberate search but purely by accident and in the most improbable place. I still shudder when I think how close we came to not finding it at all.

Behind the servants' wing stood two buildings. One of these housed the water pump and the pressure tank that supplied the buildings with water. The other, deserted, was originally an icehouse, and contained two separate rooms entered by different doors.

Icehouses were a relic of pre-refrigerator days when ice cut from nearby ponds was stored in winter in those repositories and then drawn down during the following summer, as needed by the kitchen help. The origin, probably, of the saying "That cuts no ice with me."

There was one small room, perhaps eight by eight, lined with brick, a room within a room so to speak, since it was completely enclosed save for the door to the outside and was surrounded by the room in which the ice had been stored.

The big room, within which the food section was enclosed, was a dark, damp place without windows. The sole light came from the roof that had rotted away along the ridge pole, just enough to light the place dimly. The floor was of dirt. An enormous rolltop desk, completely ruined by damp, stood in one corner; the rest of the room was full of old lumber, some Victorian valences, poles for tying up string beans, scrap lumber, and, against the far wall, an untidy stack of barrels and boxes. I had glanced inside once or twice, but had not bothered to crawl over the piles of lumber to check the barrels.

Jordy was more enterprising than I, and one day he burst into the Big House with an exultant shout. "Come quickly! I've found ten barrels in the icehouse. I think they contain china and glass. At least the top one does."

We all dropped what we were doing and rushed out to the back to see for ourselves. In an old wheelbarrow standing outside the icehouse door was a Meissen dinner plate with an exquisitely delicate rose design.

"How on earth did you find it?" someone asked.

"I don't know what made me do it, but I was just rummaging around the place and I opened the door to the icehouse. I saw the barrels in the back and something made me go over and see if there was anything in them. The one on top was empty but, when

I thumped the others with my fist, they resounded with the good, solid, sound of something inside. There are ten of them, all full!"

I scrambled inside to have a look for myself. There was a cardboard box sitting on top of one of the barrels, and, when I tried to lift it, I found it to be very heavy. Inside, I discovered an enormous onyx mantel clock in the shape of a Greek temple with gilt columns and an enameled face in pale green. The delicate filigreed gilt hands and the other gilt ornaments on the clock were untarnished, and the clock looked in perfect condition.

Hastily, I carried it out to the sunlight, where the glistening gilt and bright colors stood out in improbable contrast against the rough wood of the wheelbarrow on which I had set it down. I returned to the inside of the icehouse and found two other mantel ornaments inside the same box, a pair of onyx and gilt urns that were apparently part of the onyx clock fireplace mantel set.

It took us all a few minutes to collect our wits, so impressive was Jordy's find. No one, we agreed, leaves valuable china and bric-a-brac in an icehouse whose roof is falling in. By what chance had these barrels and the clock mantel set been placed in one of the few corners of the icehouse where the roof was whole?

By good luck, the servants' dining room was temporarily empty of trash because we had taken it out to the Burning Ghat the day before. We dragged tables from the kitchen and set up an assembly-line unpacking operation. Jordy, Lloyd, and I removed the neatly wrapped packages from the barrels and carried them out to Katherine and Louise. The latter unwrapped them and put them on the tables, keeping matching pieces together.

After a few trips, we became impatient with carrying the packages in our arms and pressed the old wheelbarrow into service. For several hours we worked, unpacking hundreds of little tissue-paper packages from the bone-dry excelsior in the barrels and loading them into the old wheelbarrow for their journey to the house. Louise and Katherine stood by the tables inside the servants' dining room, where they carefully unwrapped our fantastic finds.

Fantastic they were indeed. The original find, the Meissen plate, came from a complete set of a dozen each of dinner plates, butter plates, luncheon plates, cups and saucers, platters, and vegetable dishes, as well as other dishes of a special nature we could only guess at, relics of a more formal age of servants and service.

We had no understanding of one of our best findings. It appeared to be a rather lovely, simple, off-white Oriental porcelain bowl, perhaps from which to serve salad. We liked it, gave it the normal care accorded a nice piece of porcelain, and placed it on the table in the servants' dining room.

Visitors admired its simple shape, handled it, and put it back on the table in the China Room. This went on all summer. None of us wanted it for our own; when we came to sell things later in the summer, it proved to be not porcelain as we thought, but white jade.

There was a small wooden crate that was separate from the barrels in the icehouse. When we opened it, we found that it contained an oriental box covered in brocaded linen and equipped with a concealed sliding top. When we had figured out the combination, we slid the panel aside and found an exquisitely carved oriental box of sandalwood, about two feet long and one foot wide. Almost every inch of the box was covered with delicately carved little figures, buildings, foliage, and trees carved in relief. The box must have been made in the Orient on order, for, worked into the design on the top was the letter *S* and the Schuchardt coat of arms, its gross outlines contrasting sharply with the delicacy of the oriental designs surrounding it. We figured that it must have been intended as a jewel box but never completed for the person who originally ordered it. We were really in luck on this one because, though china and glass could survive wet and winter's freeze and thaw, dampness would have warped the box completely out of shape, irretrievably ruining the delicate oriental carving.

Our other finds ran from delightful little perfume bottles decorated with nosegays of varicolored flowers done in glass, to a set of earthenware salad plates in the shape of oak leaves, to three-foot-high cranberry glass vases ornamented with a profusion of gilt, as well as ornate objects of even greater Victorian hideousness, including a porcelain pug dog.

By that time, we realized that the erstwhile China Room was too small, and we renamed the servants' dining room the China Room. The next day, we took all the antique materials Katherine and I had stored in the room upstairs and moved them there.

We then turned the adjacent kitchen into an informal Gift Room. There were many little pieces of bric-a-brac of various kinds: ashtrays, little cream pitchers, kitchen utensils such as serving spoons and fruit knives, items of no value to us. Whenever visitors came by, and there were many of them, each could take one of these little objects away with them as a memento. Little girls were especially enthusiastic over tiny embroidery scissors suitable for a doll's house, as well as stores of silk and velvet ribbon that dated from Christmas celebrations before the Crash.

The mystery of how the barrels got there in the first place pursues me to this day. Among our earlier finds had been several Canton vegetable dishes without tops that were sitting in the butler's pantry adjacent to the kitchen; tops that matched some of the vegetable dishes were later found in the icehouse. From this, we deduced that the barrels must have been placed in the icehouse by mistake and forgotten. Wherever and whenever they had been packed, the vegetable dishes and their tops were separated and packed in different barrels. Sometime, perhaps in 1921, when my cousins moved to Open Country, and in the confusion of the move, the barrels were ordered placed in the icehouse to get them out of someone's way and then forgotten by all concerned. Who can tell? It had all happened forty years before.

A few days after the discovery of the antiques in the icehouse, we received a letter from Mr. Quinn, the lawyer I had met right after I came east, announcing an appointment for us to see the silver and other things that Cousin Margaret had in storage in New York.

None of us had any idea what these might be. We knew from old bills that had come to light that a great many things had been in storage in the Lincoln Warehouse as well as in Manhattan Storage in the mid-thirties, and that our little cousin had been forced to sell many of them to meet overdue storage bills. Just what might be left, however, we had no idea because we had found no up-to-date inventories.

At the same time, we got a phone call from Lewis Rubinstein. He said that he was very busy and could not stay long but asked if he might bring over a friend, Timothy Trace, who, he said, was an authority on antique furniture. He said further that he wanted Trace to look over some of our pieces. He also said that Trace was an authority on books, and might be able to give us an estimate of the value of the books on the living room bookshelves.

The two of them came over the following morning. Trace was not a prepossessing man. Heavyset and tall, in his mid-fifties, he had a florid face, iron-gray hair, a snaggle-toothed smile, and a rasping voice. He spoke, however, with evident authority, and he was not afraid to list his reasons for his conclusions about our furniture and books.

The books, he said, were a "reader's library" and would bring very little. There were a few books that might interest collectors, but very few, and even these would not bring very much. A hundred dollars maybe, he said, but not much more.

He was deeply impressed with the Chippendale mirror in the downstairs hall. "A bit large," he said. "Without the finial, it must be seven feet tall, and the finial would probably add another foot-and-a-half to two feet on top of that. Even so, it might bring a couple of thousand dollars if you could locate the finial."

"Oh, yes," I responded. "A friend, Jordy Jack, spoke of it when he came through."

Trace went on without responding to my comment.

"Those mirrors usually had some sort of bird mounted there, either a gilt phoenix or an eagle. It could be either, but I'm inclined to think it was probably a phoenix. If you can locate that, the mirror will be complete and much more valuable to a collector. Do you have any idea where it might be?"

"None whatsoever," I said. "If it is two feet high, we ought to have run across it in the house, and we haven't. Our cousin had some things in storage, and it is just possible that this might be among them. I can ask her former servants if they know anything about it."

He cautioned about being too hasty in disposing of our things, saying that antique dealers were none too scrupulous in their dealings with ignorant heirs. Like John Wainwright, Allen Matlock's friend, he advised that we learn all we could, even to the point of making a tour of some of the antique shops in New York to find out what retail prices might be like.

He also suggested that we check the American Wing of the Metropolitan Museum for pieces similar to ours on display. Through the museum experts, he said, we could get an idea of what our antiques were worth.

He then suggested that an auction might be the easiest and most profitable way of disposing of our things, and he recommended O. Rundle Gilbert as an excellent man to get in touch with. He further suggested we get in touch with Parke-Bernet Galleries in New York. Some of the furniture and bric-a-brac, he said, might be sold through antique auctions. After that, the two of them left, Rubinstein promising to come back later when he was less busy. We knew he would be back

This was beginning to look like a major project. John Wainwright had been correct in his estimate. We were indeed in a business, and the backbreaking work of unpacking might well prove to be the easiest part of the whole thing. Already confused by the multiple possibilities, I asked Trace if we could perhaps hire him as a kind of consultant and, with his advice, place some of the items of special interest, such as our Tiffany vases for example, with dealers with special interests. He said we could, and I left it at that, planning to talk to my cousins about it later.

After he left, I made a few phone calls trying to track down the missing finial. The old gardener, Matt, said he remembered hearing it discussed among the servants and said that he thought it was in the attic. The old cook, Mrs. Antoni, thought she remembered it being sent to storage. The Micciches knew nothing about it, though they volunteered the information that a man whose name they did not know had offered Cousin Margaret $5,000 for the mirror in their presence.

"Miss Leverich was furious about it," Mrs. Micciche said. "You know what she was like. She never liked anyone to know too much about her affairs. She was down visiting me when he came in. I don't remember what he looked like. I was too amused by her reaction to notice much else. She sure was funny about it."

My cousins and I combed the house the next day, but without success. We searched the attic shadows by flashlight, went over the cellar carefully the same way, and we looked on top of all the high armoires in the house, hoping it might have been put there for safekeeping.

No finial. Our only hope was Lincoln or Manhattan. Perhaps Cousin Margaret had decided it was too fragile to leave out and had stored it there.

A few days later, I went to New York for our scheduled meeting with Cousin Margaret's lawyer, Mr. Quinn, whom I had not seen since my visit with him in the Empire State Building in early summer. Since it was a nice cool day, I went in early and stopped off at Parke-Bernet Galleries. To my surprise, they seemed quite willing to send someone out to see if there was anything that might be of interest to their auction clientele.

After leaving Parke-Bernet, I walked down Madison Avenue, which had become an expensive antique row since I had last been there. I noticed a number of things for sale that were similar to some of our china and glass pieces. One shop in particular contained nothing but Tiffany Favrile glass.

My eyes bugged out when I saw the price on a vase similar to the one I had first seen in the dining room sideboard that first day. The price tag said $130. I had no way of knowing what my cousins would think, but I, myself, had no idea that that simple vase could be that valuable.

Leaving Madison Avenue, I walked over to Lincoln, where I found my cousins waiting while Mr. Quinn presented his credentials and asked to be admitted to the vaults.

I told them of my visit to Parke-Bernet and of my stroll down Madison Avenue. They seemed interested in Parke-Bernet's offer and were as surprised as I at the price asked for the Tiffany vase. Time passed, and presently we became aware that a half an hour had gone by, with no action on the part of the people behind the reception desk. We made inquiries and found that they were having trouble finding Cousin Margaret's lot of storage valuables. We discussed it briefly, and decided to go to Manhattan and return later in the hopes that they would have located her things by that time.

At Manhattan, things went more smoothly. We were taken promptly to the silver vaults and shown a small wooden crate full of silver. With the exception of a dozen eighteenth century serving spoons similar to those I had on the West Coast, there was nothing out of the ordinary. Nice mid-nineteenth century flatware and serving pieces, but nothing more.

We did have one pleasant surprise, however—two boxes of very fine lace wedding veils. I had been concerned about them, for Cousin Margaret had once told me that she had them in the attic at Open Country and, knowing the decrepit condition of the house, I had worried about them during her lifetime. To our delight, they were in perfect condition, a froth of *Point de Venice* and *Point de Rose* when unfolded from their neat packages. I could see Katherine's and Louise's eyes glisten at the thought of future family weddings in which these magnificent heirlooms could be featured.

After we had repacked the silver chest and loaded it into Lloyd and Marie-Louise's station wagon, we returned to Lincoln. They had failed to locate Cousin Margaret's belongings in our absence and seemed singularly disinterested in that failure.

As we clustered angrily about the counter questioning the man in charge, I saw something that deepened my anger. As the clerk was shuffling Cousin Margaret's file, an inventory fell open. I did not see the date, but, reading upside down, I read the words "Top of Mirror."

A sharp jab in my ribs from Katherine's elbow told me that her sharp eyes had seen the notation as well. The finial. It had to be. It was a pity that the notation was not more precise, but there was no doubt in my mind that Cousin Margaret had done what we suspected. Knowing the value of the mirror and the finial, she had packed the finial away from harm in the safety of storage.

Eagerly, we pressed the clerk for details. Why were they unable to find the Leverich lot? They had recently closed one storage warehouse, they explained, and had reshuffled the one we were in to make room for the displaced goods. It might take a few days, they said, but they were sure that they could locate our things. That was it. Temporary dead end, with our important prize almost within our grasp.

It had gotten hotter since my walk down Madison Avenue, and, steaming in the July heat and in our own stifled rage, we left. It was a little like being called to the telephone during a suspenseful mystery on television and then having to wait for the summer reruns to find out Who Done It. Sadly, the materials at Lincoln never showed up.

After we left Lincoln, Mr. Quinn said there was one more place we had to go: Cousin Margaret's safe deposit box. When we got there and Quinn had established his *bona fides*, the safe deposit box was opened and we all traipsed into a small room provided by the bank for privacy to examine the contents.

What we found there made us sick. There was a profusion of rings, bracelets, and pins, all gold or platinum set with precious stones such as diamonds, rubies, sapphires, and emeralds. The ultimate final value placed on them was in excess of $10,000. Once again, the picture of Cousin Margaret trying to saw a soup bone in half in a frigid kitchen while enough money to provide her with considerable comfort lay in her safe deposit box haunted me.

The following day, I called Tim Trace to tell him of my Madison Avenue findings. His reply impressed me as much as anything else he had said while he was in the house. "Oh yes," he said when I told him of the Tiffany Vase, "that must have been Grace Marker's. She sells only Tiffany glass."

I had taken little notice of it at the time, but, when he said the name, I remembered seeing it, gold lettering on a black background, over the door of the little shop. Tim really knew his stuff if he could identify an antique specialist that easily. No question about it, he could be of great help in getting the most for our collection, even if it cost us a fee. I resolved to make two recommendations to my cousins. First, to have Parke-Bernet come out and let us know if we had anything that would be suitable for their auctions, and, second, to hire Trace as a consultant, whatever the cost.

CHAPTER 7

You Do Have Enough Gas, Don't You?

The day after I bought the Eyesore, I got a phone call from Tengstrom. Rubinstein was back in town, he said, and he wanted to bring him over that afternoon. I checked with my cousins, and they gave their assent despite the fact that they would have left by the time Rubenstein would arrive. We agreed I should see him alone.

Late that afternoon, Tengstrom showed up with Rubenstein. I began by showing them around the house again. Rubinstein returned to the pieces that he and Trace had looked at earlier and expressed his opinions pedantically in a strident monotone.

"This highboy here," he said, looking at a double chest of drawers, "is a New York piece. I can tell that by the fluted molding running along the bottom. The brasses are original, I'm sure. We'd like to have it for the John Jay house. I don't suppose"—with a sidelong glance—"that you would be willing to give it to the museum?"

"I'm afraid not. I'd have to discuss it with my cousins, but I suspect we will be more interested in selling things. What"—with a sidelong glance of my own—"would you be willing to give us for it?"

"We've got a very limited budget. I'd say the piece was worth about twelve hundred dollars," he replied, "but I don't know if I'd be willing to pay that much."

I showed him through the entire house, including the attic. When he saw the wooden mantels, his interest quickened again.

"What do you know about these?"

"Just that they came from a house built around 1830. Most of the rest of the house is stacked near the back of the property. Why? Are you interested in them?"

"They're rather good," he said, looking at them carefully. "They're old. Here." He showed me a square nail head. "It's not a real handmade nail such as they had in colonial times, but it isn't machine-made. They're called 'cut nails' and they were made before the present method of making wire nails was developed."

"Would you like to see the old house? We call it the Newtown House because it came from Newtown, Long Island, which is now part of Queens. The house was moved up here after the property was condemned when Queens Boulevard was widened. Or, at least that is the way the family story goes. They brought it up here and stacked it in an old barn. The barn fell down finally, and the old house has been rotting there ever since."

"Are there any shutters to the house?"

"I don't know. Why?"

"The original shutters were gone from the John Jay House when the property was given to the state. I'm trying to duplicate the kind of shutters that were there when the family lived there, and I need hardware of the period. I can have reproductions made, but it is very expensive. And, besides, I'd rather have originals."

"The Newtown House wasn't built until about 1830. Are you sure we'd have the right kind of hardware?"

"Probably," he replied. "We aren't trying to restore back to the Revolution. In the first place, John Jay lived well after 1800, and in the second place, several additions that we're trying to keep were made in pre-Victorian times. I think the period would be about right. May I look at it?"

"Sure."

Together, he, Tengstrom, and I walked to the Newtown House. Lewis poked around the tangled pile of lumber, muttering to himself as he fingered the pieces that were exposed.

"Looks like you've got what I need all right," he said. "Look here. I can use some of this glass. The window frame is rotted out, but the glass has the imperfections of the 1830 period. We want to replace some of our modern plate glass with glass of the period. Here," he added, pointing to a shutter hinge that was sticking out. "This is a hand-wrought hinge. Just the kind we need. You might even find some catches in there. We need catches, doorknobs, and door latches for our job. You don't happen to have a box lock, do you?"

"What's a box lock?"

"I'm sure you've seen them in old houses. It's a lock that fastens on the outside of the door. They were used before locks were set into the door itself. We need a number of them."

"Haven't seen one yet, but one might turn up," I lied. I now understood the odd catches that Katherine and I had found when going through the barrels in the second-floor room in the Big House. For the moment, I had no intention of letting Rubinstein know that I had, in fact, unearthed some box locks.

My long-term interest in the Newtown House was finally going to be satisfied. I had wanted to dig into that pile since I first learned about it as a child. Maybe this was my chance.

The next day, I told my cousins about Rubinstein's visit, of his request for the double chest of drawers and the price he had put on it, and of what he had said about the Newtown House. Lacking my thirty-five-year store of curiosity, my cousins were a little doubtful about tearing down the Newtown House pile, but very happy about the value placed on the chest.

"I'm glad he thinks it's worth that much," commented Katherine, "but I'm afraid he'll have to look through his budget for the funds if he wants it," she added dryly. "Right, cousin?"

I agreed. I felt sure our little cousin would prefer to see us either use her furniture ourselves or get the best possible price for it.

Our first attack on the Newtown House was aborted abruptly. Jordy and I went down one day and started to clamber over the top to figure out how best to attack it. There were bundles of old shingles laid over the top and we made a start by tossing these down to the ground below.

Suddenly, Jordy jumped and cried out in pain. He had been stung by a yellow jacket. We couldn't see any of them flying around, but obviously there were one or more nests hidden in the wood beneath us. Hastily, we got down and returned to Cousin Margaret's apartment to find a remedy. Fortunately she was old fashioned enough to keep a bag of Reckett's Paris Bluing, my own family's sovereign remedy for such stings, and we applied it to his ankle while we discussed what to do next.

The obvious thing was to fumigate the pile, but this simple solution presented some rather large problems. The pile was about thirty feet on a side and stood probably fifteen feet high. What kind of a tarpaulin would be large enough to cover that? And what kind of stuff should be use? Spray cans of DDT would cost a mint and might not penetrate far enough into the pile to do any good. There was no way of telling how many yellow jacket, wasp, or bee colonies might be hidden there, or how deep they would have burrowed into the pile to make their homes.

The next day, I went to the nearest town, Ridgefield, to find out from the local hardware store what I might do about our unwelcome guests. They supplied me with a couple of cans of potassium cyanide, together with stringent warnings about its potency, and with an enormous roll of plastic that was twelve feet wide.

I took my deadly supplies back to Open Country and proceeded to scatter the cyanide down into the cracks as much as possible. I threw the contents of a second can deep under the pile. Unwinding the hundred-foot-long sheet of plastic, I wrapped the pile in what must have been the world's largest snood. It was tricky stuff and kept slipping down from the top and forcing me to climb up again to reaffix it, risking both the deadly fumes of cyanide and a repeat of Jordy's unfortunate experience of the day before.

Finally, I finished—the pile looked ridiculously like some enormous Christmas package with the transparent plastic glistening in the sun like cellophane and gently undulating in the breeze. I successfully stifled the temptation to tie a large bow somewhere and left it there for a couple of days to allow the cyanide to do its work.

A few days later, I started to remove the plastic covers from around the Newtown House. I climbed cautiously over the pile without finding or hearing any yellow jackets or hornets, though I did receive a brutal testament to the strength of the poison I had used. I picked up a heavy shutter and, seeing some of the cyanide powder still underneath it, I let it fall, getting a dose of the powder in my face as I did so. Immediately, I felt dizzy and short of breath. I climbed hastily down from the pile and lay down on the ground to recover. Presently, the feeling passed, and I resolved to be more cautious about stirring any powder remnants in future.

A little later, Lloyd and Louise arrived, and we began to dismantle the pile. Their son, Stephen, had come up with them, and we worked for some time, Stephen and I tossing things down from the top, while Lloyd and Louise stacked them to one side.

Much to our surprise, we found, once the top layers had been stripped away, that the wood underneath was in very good condition. The movers had done a fantastically careful job of dismantling the old house. Each door, each piece of molding, each door frame, each shutter, bore a number in pencil. We even found pieces of picture molding and other ornamental trim as small as six inches in length—each with numbers showing the room and wall from which it had come.

Later in the summer, we found that the cost of the move had been $15,000, in 1923 dollars—at a time when my father had bought Lacey Green and sixty acres for $5,000. It was a crime that all this careful work on a fine old building had gone to waste, and we sincerely hoped that Rubenstein could find use for some of the pieces at least in his restoration.

After several hours of work, Lloyd and Louise began to be snowed in with wood, and the big pile really did not seem much smaller. We were running into the same problem that had dogged us in the house when we unpacked closets and trunks and found ourselves with a roomful of stuff that had to be stored somewhere.

Some of the wood was in pretty good shape, and some was not. We discussed the problem over lunch and decided that the best way was to burn the wood that was rotten or had split with age and stack the rest in neat piles by category. Actually, a lot of it was waste. We found bundles of shingles and hand-split laths—interesting historical relics, but of no earthly use—as well as a lot of doors and ornamental trim that had been close enough to the top or sides of the pile to be damaged beyond repair by the sun and rain.

After lunch, we dragged Katherine's Indian pump and all the available hoses out and began a modest fire with the shingles and laths. It was very hot, and we had already ended the morning soaked with perspiration. The shingles and laths burned with intense heat, and before long we were sweaty and dirty from the smoke. Louise retired from the fray, but Lloyd, Stephen, and I worked for the balance of the afternoon. Before long, the grass around the fire got dry and blazed up, giving us a few frantic minutes running around with hoses and the Indian pump to keep the fire from spreading.

Katherine drove in with a friend, John Garrick, during the afternoon. He expressed polite interest in our project but showed little interest in our sweaty work. She gave him a tour of the Big House and then returned to her home in Mount Kisco.

By the end of the day, we had a tremendous bed of coals and a series of small piles of shutters laid aside for Mr. Rubenstein to look at on his next visit. All of them had hand-wrought hinges on them, and many had bolts and catches as well. We had no idea what they might be worth, but we were sure Rubenstein would let us know.

The next day, Jordy joined us in the work, his great strength more than appreciated as we worked our way down through the pile to the heavier door and window frames. Thereafter, as he had done while there was major work to do in the Big House, Jordy came over every day and worked with us, hauling and burning. What we would have done without him I do not know, for he could lift things that Lloyd and I could not handle.

Rubinstein came by from time to time to check on our progress. Disappointingly enough, he was not interested in ornamental trim, though he was able to give us the names of the owners of one or two post-colonial farmhouses who might be interested. He was, however, intensely interested in hardware, brass doorknobs, the box locks that he had inquired about before and about which I had brazenly lied, as well as bolts and catches for shutters and doors. He was so persistent that he made us feel positively guilty about our inability to produce them fast enough as we dug further into the pile.

Down near the bottom of the pile, we found an increasing amount of rotten wood, and finally, at the very bottom, wood that had crumbled away to powder completely. Apparently the floor boards of the barn in which the house had been stored had rotted away completely. As we were raking and leveling the mound of rotten wood, we discovered some bricks, and we shortly managed to uncover the remains of several crates of them. They were very old, salmon-red in color, and bore no traces of any mortar on them.

We stacked them to one side, and, as we raked beneath them, we discovered something white. As we dug further, we discovered that it was marble. Evidently, some marble mantelpieces lay beneath us. We dug further, and sure enough, more pieces of marble began to emerge. Tragically, however, they had been buried too long for, though some of the pieces were white and strong, many of them were either badly stained by the rust from crates of nails that were there, or they had been rotted by the acid soil around and crumbled like wet lump sugar in our fingers.

We finally managed to piece together two complete mantelpieces of carved marble, though many of the pieces were rotted or broken, and we doubted that one mantel could be put together from the pieces that were sound. It was a heartbreaking sight. Had they been stored *above* the crates of bricks rather than beneath them, they might have survived, but the weight of the bricks above them had, over the years, forced them deep into the acid soil.

When we were finally through, we had an impressive pile of hand-wrought hinges and pintles and a few bolts, all of them from the rotted shutters. We piled them beside the large pile of shutters we had laid aside for Mr. Rubinstein. In addition, there were half a dozen windows, still set in their frames, complete with some handsome paneling and internal molding.

We had, in addition, a large stack of windows made of the old glass that Rubenstein had said he was interested in. There were also a number of porch columns, some pilasters in the Greek Revival style and several stacks of various kinds of picture, window, and door moldings, as well as some wood paneling that, according to the label, had come from the library of the Newtown House. We got in touch with Mr. Rubenstein, and serious bargaining over the pieces began.

"What do you want for them?"

"We don't know really," I replied. "What would you be willing to pay for them?"

Rubinstein picked up one of the hinges in a discouraged manner and turned it over in his hand.

"I don't really know," he said. "I've got a pretty tight budget. It would cost me a buck to have duplicates made, but then again these are in pretty bad shape. We'd have to work on them to take the rust off. You know, of course," he said, looking over his glasses. "You can't get anything for those from a junkie."

This was not going to be as easy as I had thought. We had hoped that Rubinstein would tell us, in plain terms, what the hinges and other things were worth and let us have it. He knew what it would cost him to have duplicates made, and he also knew that, if we didn't sell to him we weren't going to sell to anyone.

"I wish you'd set a price on these," he said. "Then I'd tell you whether I would be willing to pay it or not."

"How can we?" I countered. "We have no idea what they are worth. We want to be fair, but we have no way of knowing what 'fair' is. All we want is a fair price, but if we set a price on them we have no way of knowing whether it is fair or not."

"I've got my problems too," he whined. "If I pay too much for these things, the State will be on my back. I'm over budget already in the restoration, and I don't want to get into trouble. This is the first major restoration I've done."

Finally, after more dispirited haggling, during which both of us claimed that we lacked any basis for placing a value on the hinges, we struck a bargain based on one-half of the cost of having the restoration hinges made to order. Characteristically, Rubenstein was unhappy about the results of the bargain, or at least seemed so, and I was unable to figure out whether we had made a decent bargain or not.

The subject of the glass came up for discussion next, with no more satisfactory results. He hemmed and hawed about prices and size, compared our discussed price with the price of modern plate glass and size, and we finally settled on a price of fifteen cents a pane. It was not a happy afternoon, and we ended up disliking Mr. Rubenstein rather strongly for his refusal to lay his cards on the table in a more frank manner. Still, we had gotten better than $250 for what he had taken from the Newtown House, which—if we did not count our many days of backbreaking labor with Jordy's help—was a pretty good return on the twenty-five dollars' worth of poison and plastic that I had originally invested in the project.

From the Newtown House, we returned for another tour of

the Big House. Mr. Rubenstein expressed his by now usual hope that we would donate the big New York highboy and asked if we would be willing to give some of the dresses to the Jay House. He also showed interest in some enormous flour sifters in the kitchen, a tole kettle and stand, and a Victorian tin bathtub and examined the box locks that we had found in the China Room. He obviously wanted them but, as usual, insisted that we place a price on them. This time, we reached a complete standstill, and he left, complaining about our failure to locate additional hardware for the great stack of doors we had found in the Newtown House. He also gave us the distinct impression that he suspected us of having secreted those away in hopes of getting a better price for them from some antique dealer. Which, strictly speaking, was what I had done since I had "forgotten" to mention the box locks Katherine had found when were rummaging around in the upstairs bedroom we had unpacked shortly before.

While we were still embroiled in the Newtown House, Bennet had called me to suggest that I come with them to a charity ball at the local country club. She had arranged a blind date for me, a girl who was coming up from New York to spend the weekend.

"Sorry, Bennet, you know perfectly well I don't have a tuxedo with me. I don't even have a pair of black shoes here."

Bennet chuckled. "I'm not going to let you get off that easily. I've already arranged for something for you to wear, and surely you can dye a pair of brown shoes black, can't you? I was talking to Janet about this, and she told me that you had given a white linen jacket to Andrzej several years ago and he still has it.

"He'd be delighted if you'd use it, and you can wear almost any dark trousers with it. The Country Club will be dimly lit, and no one will know the difference. I'm not taking 'No' for an answer. Be here at seven on Friday for cocktails. Good-bye." The phone went dead.

I knew when I was licked. The closest thing I had to dress shoes was a pair of Mexican ankle-length riding boots that I dyed black.

Providing I kept my trouser cuffs down, no one would notice—I hoped. I picked up my old white jacket from Janet and borrowed a black tie and pleated dress shirt from Andrzej.

Friday night, dressed in my borrowed and made-over finery, I wound a brightly striped Italian silk stole from the Big House ("Bought by MDL in Naples during her trip to Italy, Egypt, and the Holy Land in 1909"), stuck a rose from the fence by the icehouse into my lapel, and sallied forth to Bennet and Jordy's house in the Eyesore.

When I arrived, Bennet met me at the door with a long face.

"You'll have to go with Ora alone," she said. "Ellen has the pip and I don't want to leave her, and Jordy isn't even here. He went to New York today and he can't get back. The transmission went out when he was on the Merritt Parkway, and he had to walk two miles to find a phone. He's still in a garage in South Norwalk."

When I told her I thought the whole thing was trumped up and that she was a coward for not going with me in my pretend tuxedo, she laughed mischievously and took me to meet my date. Privately, I thought she rather relished the whole situation, especially as I would now have my blind date in the Eyesore, their jeep being completely out of the question. Heaven knows the Eyesore was bad enough, but the jeep was just as dirty as my truck and far less comfortable. I had driven it to New York once, earlier in the summer, and very nearly required the attention of a kidney specialist afterward.

Ora was short, with dark hair and eyes. She seemed shy beside Bennet's ebullience, and most of the conversation over cocktails was between Bennet and myself. Ora wore silver slippers and a pale blue bouffant dress with many layers of fine tulle over a silk underskirt. I wondered what I could do to protect that delicate material from the rusty floor of the Eyesore and how this quiet girl would react to going to a formal dance in a battered truck.

As I sat on the Jacks' low couch, my hopes of keeping the tops of my boots hidden by my trousers were shattered immediately, for my cuffs eased immediately above my boots, exposing both my boots and bright sports socks beneath them. I saw Ora steal a surprised glance at my feet and caught Bennet, eyes sparkling with fun, stifling a snicker at my situation.

Ora sipped her drink in almost total silence, and, when she was through, Bennet provided me with sheets to cover the seat and floor of the Eyesore. When I took Ora out to the truck, she at least had something clean to sit on and put her feet on. It was just after sunset when we left the Jacks' for the ten-mile drive to the dance.

After helping her into the truck and settling her bouffant skirts so that I could shut the truck door, I climbed into the driver's side, only to find that her skirt had flowed over the floor-mounted gearshift lever. I started the truck, threw out the clutch and started to grope in the darkness for the gearshift.

"I hope you find what you are looking for under that skirt," she said. I laughed and turned toward her, expecting to find a friendly twinkle in her eyes. Instead, I found her face frozen at her inadvertent *double entendre*, her eyes fixed on the skirt at her feet. I found the gearshift lever, and we drove out of the Jacks' driveway in uncomfortable silence. (This was in the early 1960s, pre-Pill, when good girls didn't "do it" before they were married. A very innocent age.)

Halfway to the dance, I turned off onto a side road, a shortcut familiar to me from my childhood. Hardly had we left the main road when the headlights suddenly went out without warning, leaving us in total darkness on a lonely road.

I knew I had a store of fuses because this had happened before. When I first bought the truck, a pair of hefty blinker lights had been installed on the front and rear fenders to make the truck conform to New York State vehicle laws, and these had apparently caused some sort of overload because, when I turned the turning indicator knob on or off at night, the headlights sometimes blew their fuse. It made no sense to me, for the new turning indicators were not affected by the blown fuse. I had taken the Eyesore back to Tator's Garage, where they claimed they had fixed it.

After getting a fuse out of the glove compartment, I swung my head down near Ora's lap where I could replace the blown fuse. Suddenly, like a chill breeze about my shoulders, I became aware of a frozen silence from the still figure above me. Hastily, I explained what I was doing. She seemed somewhat, but not entirely, convinced when the headlights went on again.

"You do have enough gas, don't you?" was all she said, and we drove in constrained silence punctuated by two more blown fuses before we reached our destination. Since my supply of fuses was now down to two, I stopped at a gas station to buy more fuses if possible and to fill up with gas. I wanted no more problems than I already had.

The gas station attendant made no secret of the fact that he was vastly puzzled at the sight of two people in evening dress in a rusty old truck, and he kept looking at Ora while he was gassing the truck and hunting up a box of fuses for me. Ora sat like a frozen statue under his gaze and wouldn't even look at me when I climbed back into the truck to drive the remaining half mile to the Country Club. She seemed immensely relieved when I helped her out of the truck at the club door and went to park.

As I walked back into the clubhouse, I saw her just coming back from a phone booth, where I assumed she had been calling Bennet for reassurance. I pretended not to notice, and together we went in for cocktails before dinner. Whatever Bennet told her must have restored a measure of her faith and a pre-dinner cocktail finished the job, for she loosened up and finally began to laugh.

"I keep thinking of that kid in the gas station," she said. "I wonder what kind of tales he'll tell about us when he gets off work tonight. You and me in evening dress and that dreadful old truck of yours—rummaging through his spare parts drawer for fuses for those irresponsible headlights of yours!"

The rest of the evening was pleasant, and we were both in high spirits when the dance came to an end and we prepared to return to Bennet's. This time, I decided to stick to the main road, even if it was longer, and we drove gaily along, stopping every now and then to replace a fuse. By now, it had almost become a game with us.

Unfortunately, there were no gas stations open at that hour of the morning, and long before we were home, my last fuse gave out.

"Now what do we do?" Ora asked.

"Well, it'll take time and I'll have to take back roads to avoid the police," I said, "but we can make it. There is a switch that makes all four turning lights blink on and off as a warning if you're parked. We can't go very fast, but, if I turn that on, I'll get a kind of off-again-on-again view of the road in front of us and we should have no trouble."

Once again, I turned off the main road and made my way cautiously down a twisting country lane, my makeshift headlights giving occasional warnings of trees, sharp curves and other obstacles in our path. Fortunately, the State Police were sticking to the main roads that night, and we got back to Bennet and Jordy's without incident.

Bennet was still up, and Jordy had returned from his own automotive adventures when we got back. Bennet's eyes were sparkling when she met us at the door.

"You must have had a hot time on the telephone," I said when Ora had gone to put her corsage in the refrigerator.

"Oh, you know about the phone call?"

"Ora didn't tell me, but I saw her coming out of a phone booth when I came into the Club after parking the truck. I figured she was either calling you or a taxi."

"I'm here to tell you," Bennet said, "it wasn't easy. She was all ready to call a taxi, but I told her you were a harmless nut, and she agreed to stick it out through the dance and see what happened. I figured it would be all right once she got to know you a little better."

Jordy burst into laughter and refused to be impressed with my protestations of innocence.

"I've got to give it to you, Russ," he said, "you're original at least. Running out of gas is old hat—blown fuses is at least a new approach," he continued with a great boom of laughter.

Vandals or no vandals, I was in no mood to drive back to Open Country that night, and I spent the night at the Jacks'. The following morning, with fire in my eyes, I drove down to Tator's Garage to have the lights fixed.

While the mechanic was chasing down the problem, I fell into conversation with some of the men hanging around the garage.

"Understand you're from the old Leverich place," one of the men said.

"Yes," I replied, "the old place is quite a mess."

"I hear the old lady had some pretty nice things up there," he replied. "You found some china hidden away in the icehouse didn't you?"

"As a matter of fact, we did," I admitted, wondering how the news about our find had gotten around the neighborhood. I wasn't surprised that local people were curious about the old place. Cousin Margaret must have been something of a local character in her later years, and of course there would have been talk when the police were called to investigate the theft of the Wedgwood before she died. But this talk about the icehouse was different. We hadn't talked about it locally, and I was sure that Jordy hadn't either because he was as conscious of the dangers of vandalism and theft as we were.

"I'll tell you one thing," I said, "that's a ghostly old place to sleep in. I'm getting used to it now, but I still leave a few lights on when I go to bed." If there was to be talk about the place, I wanted to make it publicly plain that there was someone in the house at night as well as during the day. The truck, which I always parked near the kitchen door, would add substance to this impression.

By that time, I had spent much more time at Open Country than I had originally expected, and had to leave for a week to deal with some issues on the West Coast. I departed, assuring my cousins that I would return as soon as possible.

CHAPTER 8

This Is Going to Be a Very Important Sale

While I was gone, Lloyd and Louise stayed in Cousin Margaret's apartment during the week as custodians. The first time I saw them on my return they seemed relieved to have me back. Katherine was the same.

"I don't want to upset you, old man," Lloyd said, "but you know we couldn't stay here every night, and we think someone has been in the house."

"What makes you think that?"

"Little things we couldn't put our fingers on," Katherine said. "There were times when we found closet doors open—doors we all thought we had left closed—and I can't explain it, but somehow the place did not always seem quite the same as when we left it. Nothing we could put our fingers on."

When Jordy came over that day, he was equally concerned. "I called the house one day to find out when you would be back. Someone—a man—answered the phone. Then he hung up. Lloyd said he wasn't there that day, and neither was Katherine."

Fortunately, I have a photographic memory that had, up to that time, enabled me to remember almost any item in the house once it had been unearthed and put in its assigned spot. I went over to the Big House to see if anything seemed to be missing.

There was no question about it. Someone had been there. The day before I left, Jordy and I had been rummaging around in the attic, and we had found a small wooden box filled with straw in the dark shadows under the eaves. The first thing my exploring fingers had found was a handsome gilt epergne ornamented with red and blue enamel. We had also found one or two boxes of fishing tackle (Cousin Henry's?) and a crate of old newspapers in the shadows, and we had decided to make a more thorough job of going through the litter in the attic after I returned from New York. A small box of carefully tied trout flies was missing, as was the epergne.

I checked with Jordy, and his memory was the same as mine. There was no doubt that someone had taken both the epergne and the trout flies. There were a few other items missing as well—a pair of crystal decanters had disappeared, as had a very nice little country-style pine chair. The chair had been a favorite of mine, and I remembered the decanters as well, for they matched a pair I had in Los Angeles.

I had made a mental note to ask my cousins if I could include them in my share when we finally came to make our division. There might be other things missing as well, but I couldn't be sure.

While I was away, Katherine had returned the ten Duncan Phyfe chairs from the dining room, as well as Grandpa Leverich's portrait, a full set of Spode china, and various other things that they had removed from the house in the early spring after other intruders had been in the house. Needless to say, everyone was glad I had returned, and I resolved to watch the house very carefully in future.

I also learned that the estate appraiser had been through in my absence, and he had completed his appraisal of Cousin Margaret's property. This meant, Mr. Quinn told us, that my cousins and I were now free to begin taking concrete steps to dispose of our inheritance.

We were, by this time, thoroughly fed up with possessions. Just as on the day of our discovery in the icehouse, we had become so tired of lugging heavy china and glass around the house that we ceased to care about their value; we had found our acquisitive instincts had been dulled by the enormous amount of material facing us, and we all agreed that we wanted to sell most of the things we had unearthed.

The easiest way to do this would have been to hold an auction in the house, but Cousin Margaret had written a clause into her will specifically forbidding an auction on the property. We were, thus, faced with the enormous problem of moving everything in the house if we were to auction it off.

We agonized over this problem for much of the remainder of the summer. We felt morally bound to observe Cousin Margaret's dictum, and, in addition, my cousins and I, as executors, were bound by law to ensure that the provisions of her will were carried out. At the same time, we were reasonably sure that she was unaware of the problem that she had presented to us and that she had been close enough with a buck in her lifetime that she would not have wanted to see money wasted in needless moving charges.

To make our problem worse, every knowledgeable person had advised an auction and many of them, like Tim Trace, had mentioned O. Rundle Gilbert as the best man for the job, since he handled similar auctions in that part of Westchester County. Jordy, indeed, had given us a printed brochure on his latest auction.

Ignoring my suggestions regarding Parke-Bernet and Tim Trace, however, Katherine had, in my absence, gotten in touch with Samuel Alpert, an auctioneer in White Plains she claimed had done a lot of work appraising for both Parke-Bernet and the Metropolitan Museum of Art in New York.

She had brought him up to the house to look over the contents, and some of his estimates exceeded our wildest dreams. For the bow-front bureau Jordy had admired, he claimed he could probably get $2,000, and he valued the Chippendale mirror at about $5,000 if we could find the finial.

Katherine was enthusiastic about him. "He won't touch a house where the contents won't bring at least ten thousand dollars," she said. Lloyd and Louise were noncommittal, never having met him. I was intrigued, though a little suspicious, largely because I had faith in Jordy's judgment by this time, and he doubted very much that Alpert could get what he claimed. Frustratingly enough, he had had to go into the hospital for a minor operation and could not return for about two weeks, so all we could do was wait in the meantime.

That was annoying, but all we could do for the moment. As a matter of fact, were to spend much of the rest of the summer waiting for something to happen. Somehow, there were always delays. In this case because Alpert was sick. Later appointments always seemed to be "next week," or (worse) "next week, maybe." In the meantime, the remainder of the summer slipped by while we agonized over evaluation and reevaluation of the value of our inheritance and over decisions about the best way to dispose of it

A few days later, Katherine called to say that Alpert was then well enough to see us, and that he had made an appointment to meet at her house that afternoon. I was delighted, having begun to chafe at the delay, and I was anxious to meet the man who had claimed to be able to get some handsome prices for our inheritance.

Alpert was late, and we were relaxing over drinks when his car pulled into the driveway. When Katherine opened the front door to let him in, her large frame hid him completely, and we only heard the thin, reedy voice of an old man apologizing for his lateness in a strong Lower East Side New York accent. When he came into view, we saw that he was short, spare, and bald with a confident, almost fatherly air about him.

His eyes were bright, and, as he cast quick, birdlike glances about the room, we could almost see him adding up the value of the handsome antiques with which Katherine's living room was furnished. He was bent with age and seemed almost to disappear into the large, comfortable chair that Katherine provided for him, but he spoke with authority. I could not help but compare him with some Indian guru surrounded by his younger students, forming a mental image of Lloyd, Louise, and I, clustered about his feet like religious followers, eager to receive the information he had to give us. Katherine sat back with the relaxed air of one who had produced the promised rabbit from the hat.

We learned very quickly that the word "Important" looms large among antique dealers and their clients. Outlining his qualifications for us as newcomers to his world, he spoke of Important dealers he knew, Important auctions he had conducted and Important pieces he had secured for Important collectors. He was, by inference, too discreet ever to mention names, and we also learned quickly that the antique business is highly secretive by nature. To be Important, we gathered, one really should have a cloak, a mask (and perhaps a sword), and, most Important, an unlisted telephone number.

He had already, he told us, gotten in touch with some Very Important dealers who were breathlessly awaiting a chance to view Open Country's priceless collection of treasures.

"This is going to be a Very Important sale," he said, "and I want to get bids in advance from some of the Important dealers. After I find out what they have to say, I can give you a better idea of what we can realize." He paused, and I noted that he had glanced at each of us in turn, with raised eyebrows, as he spoke. "Of course, you realize that it is to my advantage to get as much as possible because that increases my commission." It looked as if we had someone genuinely in our corner, which was heartening.

We discussed with him the problem of Cousin Margaret's injunction against holding an auction on the property. He deferred action on that problem until he had a better idea of what the market might be for our merchandise, a phrase that jarred us all somewhat since it sounded disrespectful in some way to our little cousin.

We accepted his suggestion of letting him arrange for dealers to come and take a look, and we closed the discussion on that note. After he left, Lloyd, Louise, and I agreed that we were deeply impressed by him.

The following day, he phoned us at Open Country to tell us of the arrangements he had made, all of which were highly secretive. He mentioned no names and told us that it was most important that none of the dealers know that any of their competitors were being invited up, or they might refuse to come. Evidently, each of them was to be left with the impression that he (or she) alone was in on the ground floor.

The schedule was worked out with something approaching stopwatch timing. I was to pick up the first Very Important Man at Alpert's shop in White Plains, some thirty miles away, the following morning at 9:00 sharp, and then I was to drive him to Open Country for his tour of the house. As soon as we were ready to leave, and this must be no later than 11:30, I was to phone Alpert secretly and let him know we were ready to leave.

He would then dispatch another Important dealer, to be met by Lloyd and Louise, while I ferried dealer number one back to White Plains. My two cousins were to dispose of dealer number two by no later than 2:00 p.m. so that Alpert could schedule yet a third individual for an afternoon tour. After each one had seen the house and his contents, they would phone him, and he would let us know later what they had to say.

So secretive was this operation that Alpert even instructed us on which parkways to use so that he could send the second and third teams via different routes with no danger of anybody seeing and recognizing anybody else while en route. It all seemed more than a little extreme, but Alpert issued such stringent instructions that we figured he knew what he was doing. Anyhow, he was Authority, and we were, by this time, sufficiently confused that we were willing to accept Authority's instructions, no matter how screwy they might seem.

The following morning, I arrived at Alpert's antique shop in

White Plains on time. The shop bore out our estimate of Alpert because, though small, it was filled with fine marquetry and mahogany furniture, and the ceiling was ablaze with crystal chandeliers. It was obvious that he dealt in high quality, if flashy, antiques.

Alpert led me to the back of his office, where he introduced me to a disappointingly ordinary man in a gray business suit who looked vaguely familiar. He introduced him as Gerald Levy of the firm of Ginsberg and Levy. I immediately felt somewhat like a traitor, for Mr. Levy and I had had some pleasant and apparently entirely fair dealings some years before over the sale of some family miniatures.

We spent no time in conversation, and I took Mr. Levy outside for the trip to Open Country. He eyed the Eyesore doubtfully and said that he would drive his own car, allowing me to show him the way. He was polite but firm, explaining something about wanting his own car because he had other appointments in that part of Westchester County.

Since this was not According To The Plan, I had some nervous moments, for it meant that I was losing a measure of control over his movements and could not—should he want to stay longer than the schedule called for—plead that we had to leave because of some appointment of my own. Worse still, Alpert was by now back inside his shop so I could not warn him that his delicately balanced operation was out of kilter.

Even the weather seemed against me. I had risen to face lowering clouds, and, as I rode out of White Plains, it began to rain in earnest. This meant that the house would be colder and drearier than normal and the light too poor to show off all our things to decent advantage.

After we arrived, Mr. Levy and I had a cup of coffee together before beginning our tour. He was an agreeable conversationalist, and I felt thoroughly relaxed by the time we left Cousin Margaret's apartment for the Big House. Mr. Levy had seemed so very frank and open with me during our dealings over my miniatures that I felt sure he would be equally frank and open in telling me what he thought of what we had for sale.

I was wrong, however. Once inside the house, he clammed up completely. We walked through the house in almost total silence, while he opened drawers and upended them, pulled pieces of furniture out from the wall to inspect the backs, looked carefully at brass handles, upended chairs to check them, and inspected fire irons, china and glass, all without comment.

I followed him with growing concern, standing first on one foot and then the other while holding the flashlight so that he could see in the gloom. I helped him move furniture and told him what little I knew about the various things he was looking at. At the conclusion of our tour I was both puzzled and angry—and wondering just how honest he had been with me over the miniatures.

I was beginning to be disturbed on another level as well. My cousins and I had approached our task at Open Country from the standpoint of love. We had been fond of our little cousin in different ways, we had known her in different milieus and in different ways, and we had sorrowed over the ruin that the once beautiful home she and Cousin Catherine had shared had become. Up to that time, save for our dealings with Mr. Rubinstein, which did not involve the Big House at all, we had had uniformly pleasant interactions with those authorities who had seen the house. My friend Alan Matlock and his friend Wainwright had been respectful of our inheritance, and Tim Trace had been downright helpful. Suddenly, the atmosphere had changed. The personal response to the house that I was accustomed to was no more. There was a chill in the air, and it distressed me.

Levy did not take long to go through the house, and when he was through, we walked back to Cousin Margaret's apartment. Outside the house, his tongue loosened, and he talked chattily about the weather, the condition of the house and of its former grandeur, talking about everything, in fact, but the things he had come to see. When he finally left, I knew no more than I had in the beginning.

As soon as he left, I phoned our Fagin friend in White Plains to tell him the discouraging tale of Levy's visit. To my surprise, Alpert seemed quite happy with my report. "I know how to handle Levy," he said. "He'll be phoning me today or tomorrow and I'll let you know what he had to say."

Important Man Number Two was unable to make it that day, he said, so, wondering what More Important Matters could have forced him to cancel out, I settled down to wait for Important Man Number Three and for my cousins.

My cousins arrived first, and questioned me eagerly about Mr. Levy's reaction. They were as puzzled and annoyed as I had been at my negative report. More and more, it began to seem as if we were wandering in someone else's jungle.

Shortly after lunch, our second visitor drove into the driveway. He introduced himself as John Walton, a name I recognized from advertisements in a copy of *Antiques Magazine* that Jordy had once shown me. Walton was a young man, the son, he said, of the Walton whose ads I had seen. He had a ready charm and, over coffee, he regaled us with amusing stories of his life in the antique world. My cousins and I exchanged happy glances as we left for the Big House, confident that at least we were going to learn something concrete.

Over at the Big House, Walton justified our happy mood. He was as professional as Levy had been in his careful examination of the furniture, and he kept up a running fire of comments as he worked. He praised Grandpa Leverich's portrait and told us that it was painted on Tulip wood, which identified it as the work of one of two well-known artists of the period. The dining room chairs, he said, might have come from the shop of Duncan Phyfe himself and, if so, were very valuable indeed. He identified one small chair as a Chippendale piece, called our attention to two eighteenth century tables that we had not noticed especially before and spoke willingly of various other pieces as well. We exchanged jubilant glances during his monologue and happily followed him back toward his car.

He refused a second cup of coffee, and as we clustered about him in the rain, we learned that his firm was not interested in any of the things he had praised so highly. Of course, this left wide open the fact that he had noted a number of other things in the house about which he had kept silent.

His parting remarks, were perhaps the most damaging to our collective state of mind. There was, he said, an informal syndicate of New York antique dealers who, though in competition with each other, frequently combined to keep down the price of collector's items that appeared on the market.

If, he said, a particularly choice piece was due to come up at auction, these dealers would decide by lot who was to bid on it so that there would be no competitive bidding between them. Then, once the piece had been auctioned off publicly, they would hold a second, private, auction among themselves, away from the dangerous atmosphere of open competitive bidding.

Discovery of this dark conspiracy unnerved us all and made us feel all the more that we had been propelled into someone else's jungle. We thanked him for being so frank and retired upstairs for a much-needed drink.

There was now no doubt in our minds that our inheritance was valuable, but it was equally obvious that it was going to be very difficult for us to judge the most profitable way to dispose of it. We had all assumed that reputable dealers would deal with us in a fair and open manner, and it was becoming equally obvious that, like Rubenstein, they were not prepared to do so.

Alpert seemed to be our only reliable contact in this mysterious business. We agreed among ourselves that it was in his interest to get top dollar for our inheritance since his fee was based on a percentage of the total, and that, therefore, we could count on him to act in our interest and to protect us from our own ignorance.

Next day, we called Alpert to find out what our two visitors had told him. He had, he said, been unable to talk to both of them, but he had arranged for yet another dealer to visit us. Her name, he said, was Florene Maine.

Florene Maine was another name I recognized from *Antiques Magazine*. She was a local dealer with a very fine reputation. Friends told me that she had been one of those who had contributed to the refurbishing of the White House when Jackie Kennedy was involved in the project. I took another look, this time at the quality of her advertising and came to the conclusion that she was a businesswoman of the highest quality.

Katherine was unable to drive up the next day, but Lloyd agreed to come up and help me show her through the house. About ten o'clock, he and I heard a car outside, and we stuck our heads out of the window. Our hearts fell, for the car was an old Chevy, weather-beaten and dented. This could not be the distinguished Mrs. Maine, and we were in no mood for casual visitors.

The window on the driver's side rolled down, and a middle-aged woman with unkempt hair stuck her head out.

"This the Leverich place?" she asked in a shrill tone.

"Yes it is," I replied. "What can I do for you?"

"I'm Florene Maine. Sam Alpert sent me up to look at some things."

"Oh, yes, we're expecting you. Won't you come up?"

"Is there anything up there to see?" she asked.

"We're not experts. Perhaps you'd better come up and look for yourself. We wouldn't want you to miss anything."

The door opened, and Mrs. Maine got out. Save for the fact that she was dressed in modern clothes, she might have stepped right out of the orphanage in *Oliver Twist*. Her thin, sharp face was framed by a halo of unkempt hair caught in an untidy bun at the top of her head. She wore a sleazy, unpressed cotton dress and sloppy sling pumps from which her big toes and heel protruded.

Two other figures emerged from the car, twins of the Beadle

in the same Dickens novel, save for the fact that one was limping and supported himself with a cane. Both men were in florid middle age, were gray-headed, and each weighed close to two hundred pounds if they weighed an ounce. The trio made their way across the lawn and disappeared into the entrance below. Presently, we heard Mrs. Maine's whiny voice on the narrow stair encouraging her puffing escorts.

Once inside the apartment, she introduced them as the brothers Arenson "Who sometimes come with me on jobs."

"Well," she said sharply when the brief introductions were complete, "what do we have here?"

I suggested that they look for themselves since their knowledge of antiques was greater than mine. The three poked about the apartment with little enthusiasm.

"Tiffany," she said, picking up one of the lamps. "Don't deal with it. Philadelphia," she said nodding at a chair by the desk. "Chippendale. Think it's original, Ben?" she said to one of the Arensons.

Arenson bent down to examine the chair. "Umph," he said.

"Thought there was a big house here," Mrs. Maine said. "This here ain't worth the bother of coming."

"You passed the Big House on your way here," I explained.

"Thought it was deserted. We very nearly drove right back out," she said. "Will you take us over?"

In unfriendly silence, Lloyd and I escorted them over to the Big House and showed them through. If it hadn't been so infuriating, their method of communication would have been both fascinating and amusing to watch. They seemed to work entirely by mental telepathy, and it was obvious they had done a lot of work together.

In the big hall, Mrs. Maine leaned over and picked up an andiron. "Ben," she shrilled, "looky here."

Ben picked it up and inspected it carefully. "Umph," he said as he put it down again. Was he saying "Yes, it's good" or was he saying "Isn't a pity it's a copy?" Lloyd and I exchanged infuriated glances as Arenson placed the andiron back on the hearth.

This pattern was repeated in each room in the house. Mrs. Maine would either call attention to something and receive an undecipherable reply or she would go into ecstasies of praise over some "cute" little thing—bric-a-brac or furniture, something that even Lloyd and I knew was of little value. The trio tramped through the entire house including even the attic. As we walked up the disappearing staircase, I watched Arenson's huge bulk bend the unbraced stair treads above me as I followed him and wondered if I would survive being crushed should the worn steps give way.

When they had gone over the entire house, the three retired to a corner for a moment to consult, and then Mrs. Maine alone approached Lloyd and myself.

"You boys sure have an awful job on yours hands," she whined. "I don't envy you. It's too big for Alpert. He and I used to do business together, but he's getting pretty old and he's not the man he once was. You've got a lot of junk here, and he simply won't be able to do a decent job for you."

She stopped for a minute and then shook her head. "You pore boys got an awful job to dispose of all this junk. Tell you what I'll do. Alpert suggested that I give you a bid on the whole lot, and that's ezzactly wot I'm going to do.

"It's too big for me really, but the Arenson boys will help me out and we'll make do somehow. But it's much to big for you.

"Tell you what I'll also do. I'll give you six thousand dollars for the lot, and I'll even get rid of all those old dresses for you. What about it?" she said, squinting at me.

Even Lloyd's calm patience seemed almost ready to snap, for his eyes flashed briefly behind his glasses.

"If you don't mind," I said as calmly as I could, "we'd better talk this over with our third partner (thanking my lucky stairs Katherine wasn't there) and see what she says. Mrs. Wheeler wasn't able to come up today, and we can't make a decision without her."

"All right, boys," Mrs. Maine said shrilly, picking up her bag, "let me know. Come on, boys, we've got to go."

Mrs. Maine clattered out of the house, followed by her two elephantine escorts. They folded themselves back into their car, and Lloyd and I watched them without regret as they drove down the driveway.

"I say, old man," Lloyd said as the trio disappeared down the rutted driveway, "Alpert seems to have changed his mind a bit. I thought he was talking about an auction, but apparently he's thinking of selling to some dealer and taking his commission."

When I telephoned Alpert to tell him about Mrs. Maine's visit, he was furious.

"That old fool," he said. "She had no right to do that. She's trying to cheat me behind my back, that's what she's doing. I told her to go up and see if there was anything she wanted to bid on. Offered you six thousand dollars, did she? Well, I know how to handle her. Just leave it to me."

Katherine was as upset as Lloyd and I had been. Suddenly, Alpert seemed less the reliable ally he had seemed before. The jungle seemed to be closing in on us again. When I had pressed Alpert for details on what Levy and Walton had said to me, he was strangely evasive, and now, despite his vehement denials, I thought that he must have said something to Mrs. Maine about making a bid for the complete contents or she would not have done so.

At least, we now had some kind of clue as to how much our inheritance was worth, however. If she was willing to pay $6,000 in cash—and then undertake the expense of moving it—our inheritance must be worth considerably more than what she had offered. Despite her crocodile tears over our "tragic plight," we were sure she was making no charitable gesture to help us out. Either she was making a bid for the entire lot in order to pick up some special item—such as the mirror for example—figuring to break even on the minor items and clean up on that one item, or she and the Arensons would make a tidy profit funneling appropriate items through their own shops and selling the rest to lesser dealers. At least, however, we now had a rock-bottom figure on what our inheritance might be worth.

A few days later, Alpert drove up to tell us the results of his investigations. It was not a satisfactory session. He reiterated his opinion regarding the bow-front bureau and the mirror, he talked a lot about detailed arrangements that had to be made in running an auction and about his ability as an auctioneer, but he was curiously evasive about his conversations with Levy, Walton, and Mrs. Maine. Whenever we asked a direct question, he sort of slid around the outside of it and talked about something else.

Finally, he advised us to talk to Cousin Margaret's lawyer about the legal problems of holding an auction and then went his way. We did not see him again, though he telephoned from time to time until he realized it was a losing battle and stopped calling.

It was now three weeks since my return from the West Coast, and we seemed right back where we had begun. Lloyd and Louise did not mention the subject, but I found I was thoroughly annoyed by Katherine's failure to get in touch with Parke-Bernet in my absence or to follow up on my initial talk with Tim Trace. I restrained my anger in the interests of family peace and sat back to see what my cousins might have to suggest.

We were interrupted in our discussions by a phone call from Mr. Levy asking if his partner, a Mr. Ginsburg, and his wife, might come up. Levy said that Mrs. Ginsburg was a collector and a restorer of antique dresses and that she wanted to see Cousin Margaret's collection. We were not sure if we were in any way committed to pay Alpert his commission if the Ginsburgs, as we suspected, really wanted to confirm Levy's findings and if they intended to make officers on anything, but we agreed to let them come up. Deferring any further discussion until the Levys should have come and gone, my cousins left for their homes.

Later that afternoon, I also received a call from Janet Alkiewicz. Some weeks before, Andrzej's father, whose hobby was repairing old clocks, had taken the red marble clock that we had found in the downstairs hall, a black marble Tiffany clock from the mantelpiece in the hall, and the green Onyx clock we had found in the icehouse to see if he could put them in running order. They were now ticking happily and reliably in his workshop, and he wanted to return them to us. Could he do so the next day? I said of course he could, amazed at his success and grateful for the trouble he had taken to help us out.

Next morning, the Ginsburgs arrived on schedule, and Lloyd and I showed them through the house. They were an attractive, rather quiet, middle-aged couple. Mr. Levy was a mild, soft-spoken man; his wife, a lively matron of a conservative suburban mold. We showed them through the house carefully to give Mr. Ginsburg the opportunity to inspect anything Mr. Levy might have recommended to him. He showed little more than polite interest, but his wife was very enthusiastic about the dresses and did her best to persuade us to sell her some gilt costume jewelry that we had found.

After the tour was complete, Mrs. Ginsburg told us she was very interested in the dresses and offered $350 for them as a lot. She said that her hobby was collecting and restoring old dresses and that she very much wanted to add them to her collection. Lloyd and I explained that we could make no decisions without Katherine's input and promised to discuss her offer. She accepted this with good grace, and they prepared to leave.

Lloyd and the Ginsburgs left by the servants' wing, and I stayed behind to shut the front door. As I walked into the kitchen, I became aware of a disturbance at the narrow entrance to the servants' wing and hurried forward to find out what was happening.

Mr. Alkiewicz, whom Lloyd had never met, had arrived at the door just as the trio was about to leave. He wore a pith helmet on his head to protect him from the sun, and, around his shoulders, a net for catching butterflies. He was holding the onyx clock from the icehouse in his hands and, when he met the trio, he apparently had no idea which one or ones might be my cousins. While he was trying to introduce himself in his broken English and straighten out who he was, he suddenly caught sight of some special type of butterfly out of the corner of his eye. With a cry, he thrust the onyx clock into Lloyd's puzzled hands, grabbed his butterfly net, and dashed off out of sight around the corner of the house in pursuit of his precious prey.

Mr. and Mrs. Ginsberg were unnerved by this apparition and hurried to their car, evidently in a state of shock. Lloyd scuttled after them, still holding the onyx clock, explaining that he would be in touch with them about the dresses as soon as we had talked to Katherine. Finally, Mr. Alkiewicz appeared from the other side of the servants' wing, triumphant with his prey, and I managed to perform the necessary introductions.

Together, we carried the three clocks up to Cousin Margaret's apartment, where Mr. Alkiewicz reset the pendulums and gave us careful instruction about how to care for them. They remained ticking there for the remainder of the summer, never ticking or striking synchronously with each other, thus providing a nervous accompaniment to our deliberations.

With the departure of Mr. and Mrs. Ginsburg from Open Country, Mr. Alpert and his works passed from our lives. My cousins and I discussed Mrs. Ginsburg's offer for the dresses, and we decided to reject it. How Cousin Margaret would have felt about it I didn't know, but I personally felt that historical treasures such as those belonged in a museum and not in private hands. I was not sure that Mrs. Ginsberg would restore them with the same attention to authority that the Museum of the City of New York would. I did not know Mrs. Ginsberg, of course, but I doubted that she had the formal academic training that both Janet and Isabelle Miller had had, and therefore felt better about giving the dresses of the Museum of the City of New York rather than to some unknown collector.

I put it to my cousins that making such a gift to the Museum was both a civic duty and had tax advantages as well; to my relief, they saw it my way. Janet got in touch with the museum for me, and in a very few days, Margaret Stearns of the Costume Department came up. Miss Stearns was a very good sport about the truck when I picked her up at the nearby Katonah Railroad Station, and the day turned out to be one of our most pleasant at Open Country.

Janet had worked with her when she was at the museum, and she came over to see Miss Stearns's reaction to the dresses. To judge from the happy sounds we could hear, they and Louise spent an apparently ecstatic morning going over the contents of the closets in Cousin Margaret's wing. When they broke for lunch, Miss Stearns told us basically what Janet had outlined earlier in the summer. The museum would be delighted to accept the prize dresses, the two eighteenth century numbers, and the Empire dress. They would be happy also to take a number of the dresses from the 1850s, 1860s, and 1870s.

Beyond that, she was less enthusiastic. A few from the 1880s perhaps, as they were quite fine. But beyond that, no. Wondering what we would do with the rest of them, we agreed to let her take the ones she had designated.

Actually, she was better than her word. A few days later, a station wagon came up from the museum bearing Miss Stearns and two helpers. With astonishing speed and care, they packed the rustling silks and shiny satins, the brilliant velvets, and the dancing ostrich plumes into the back of the station wagon.

When they were through, Miss Stearns came to say good-bye with a pleasant smile. "I took a little more than I said I would at first. I couldn't resist. They were in such beautiful condition! I know you want them in museum hands. Would you mind if we passed these on those that we cannot use to smaller museums?"

"Not at all," I replied after getting nods of assent from my cousins. With a feeling of relief, that we had at last begun to dispose of Open Country's accumulation, we watched the museum station wagon drive out on its way to New York.

In due course, we received formal and gracious acknowledgements from the museum, but for me the greatest pleasure came that winter when I opened the museum's annual report, which was sent to us all at the end of the year. There I found "Perhaps the most outstanding gift came from Miss Margaret D. Leverich ... who gave a group of costumes made in Paris for New Yorkers ... The gift also included two rare eighteenth century dresses ..."

Thinking back to my little cousin, I felt she would have been deeply proud of her gift, and I was grateful to Janet for having helped make it possible. Actually, the experience had helped in the solution of a problem of my own. My family had had for years costumes from the 1860s, 1870s, 1880s, and 1890s sitting in trunks, and I had always felt that they belonged in a museum somewhere, but my parents had not seen it my way. After all, my father said, they belonged to his grandmother and his great-aunts. When I returned to the West Coast, I sent photographs of the dresses to Miss Stearns, who wrote back to suggest that I send them to the Costume Institute in the New York Metropolitan Museum of Art. They were accepted with alacrity, and I sent them off with a great feeling of relief.

When I returned upstairs to inspect the closets, I was conscious of a sudden sense of loss. Open Country might present an appalling challenge, but I had come to enjoy it, and I was momentarily upset at the thought if it coming to an end.

I had first seen those dresses as a child, when Cousin Margaret had shown them and other family memorabilia to me; I had worried about them when, as a man, I realized the decrepit condition of the Big House. I had enjoyed their coming to light and giving pleasure to the many people who had admired them since. Now they were gone, to good purpose it was true, but they remained within me a link with my own past, and Open Country's happier days and—as that link to the past—I regretted their departure.

With the dresses gone, my cousins and I returned to the still unsolved problem of how to dispose of the bulk of the furniture in the house. Alpert was still calling us occasionally, but, since that approach was clearly out, we began to cast about for new solutions.

At a family meeting after the dresses had gone, Katherine told us that a friend of hers had suggested that we let him phone a friend of his, a man who worked at Parke-Bernet, and ask him to look at the things in the house. Katherine gave the idea her warm support and urged its acceptance on Lloyd, Louise, and me.

"After all," she said, "they *are* the best auction house in the city. They only take the best," she went on energetically, "and we certainly ought to be confident of getting top dollar from one of their auctions."

It was now late August, and I felt strongly tempted to remind her that I had advanced the same idea two months before, but it seemed tactless, so I readily gave my assent. Lloyd and Louise did likewise.

Shortly afterward, Thomas Muldoon of Parke-Bernet came up to look at our things, bringing with him another man. By now, we were thoroughly accustomed to these professional tours and no longer hovered anxiously about. Muldoon made the usual thorough inspection, and, when no one else was watching, I noticed that the other man did some rummaging around on his own. The only positive thing we learned during the tour was the meaning of the mysterious interchange between Mrs. Maine and her cohorts regarding the brass andirons. They were fine, he said, and Parke-Bernet would be happy to include them in their choices.

When we returned to Cousin Margaret's apartment, Mr. Muldoon was ready to talk turkey. We later found that his estimates were about one-third high, but his words gave us considerable comfort at the time. Parke-Bernet would take merchandise that he expected would bring about $20,000 at auction. He could not, he said, guarantee that figure, but he said it was a fair estimate.

My cousins and I were flabbergasted. The figure he mentioned was more than we had thought the entire house contents were worth—and more than three times what Mrs. Maine had "graciously" offered Lloyd and me. Furthermore, Parke-Bernet would only take a small percentage of the things in the house. There still remained hundreds of items of lesser price and importance. Our heads fairly swam with delight.

We agreed to accept his offer, and a date was set for specialists to come up from New York. He recommended that, after his people had gone through, that we get in touch with O. Rundle Gilbert and hold an auction for the remainder. But we could not have Gilbert over until his men were through, he warned, otherwise Gilbert's nose would be out of joint because he did not have a chance at better pieces. The idea of further delay didn't appeal to us, for it was now nearly September, and the house was already losing the warmth of summer. Furthermore, of course, there remained the problem of Cousin Margaret's prohibition against an auction on the property.

About this time, we had a stroke of luck regarding the Newtown House. A number of my friends had come up to spend weekends with me at Open Country and had been fascinated by the house and its contents. It had been a great source of delight for me to take them through, for no two people reacted alike. So varied was the collection that there was something of interest for everyone who came through. With each guest, I would watch with interest to find out what facet of the collection appealed to him or her.

This weekend was no exception. I had known that particular guest, Julien Williams, for years in the gay community. A talented man, he was well-educated but country-bred, and his chief interests were dogs and horses. A talented man, a Yale graduate, he had, while in college, produced a musical play whose audio tape he had played for me once. My assessment at the time was that it was good, if amateurish.

His nickname was "Punky," which dated from his horse-racing days in Kentucky prior to going into college. He expressed polite interest in the house contents, but I could see that his heart was really not in it. Was this, I wondered going to be the one person to express no interest at all? It didn't seem possible.

"Tell me," he said after we had gone through the house, "didn't this used to be a working farm?"

"Yes, it did," I replied. "Why?"

"Could I see the outbuildings?"

"Sure," I replied, "what is left of them. They are in a pretty sorry state."

"I'd like to anyway. Farm buildings fascinate me."

We spent a rather dirty hour or so looking at the icehouse and rummaging through the barn, where we found an old buggy, cider presses, and other pieces of farm equipment; we toured the tumbledown cow sheds and pig pens; and then Julien pointed to a small group of buildings across the lawn.

"What are those?" he asked.

"Chicken houses. I've never gone down there because that part of the lawn seemed to belong to the tenants, and I did not feel I had the right to poke around. Besides, there couldn't be anything there."

"Can we go anyway?" he asked.

"I see no harm. Frank and Marion are away at work, but I don't think they'd mind."

Julien and I walked over, and Julien was happily poking around among the chicken feeders and other gear when something round in a box caught my eye. I reached in under a tangle of boards and found a box full of brass doorknobs and other hardware. The missing locks from the Newtown House? Had they been put there to keep them out of the weather when the old barn containing pieces of the Newtown House began to fall down? We later sold them to Rubinstein for better than $200, a pretty fair return for a morning's ramble with an old friend.

The incident also left me with some doubt about the Micciche family. Some time later, Frank remarked casually, "Oh, you found the hardware in the chicken coop" just as casually he had accepted the fact of our icehouse find. He seemed to know a great deal—and tell very little. I could not help but think back to my first visit with them. I had at the time praised a handsome cut-glass bowl they were using, one that was similar to one I had at home, and also similar to a set that Cousin Margaret's family had once owned and used as finger bowls.

The bowl was sitting in plain sight on the television set, full of pencils. The next time I visited the Micciches, it was gone. Why had it been removed? And now, the brass doorknobs and other hardware that had lain (been hidden?) under a tangle of boards in a chicken coop? The incident left a vaguely unpleasant feeling in the back of my mind, and the whole situation remains with me as one of the unsolved mysteries of Open Country.

The decision to sell through Parke-Bernet having been made, the time had come, my cousins and I agreed, for us to make our personal choices from the house. The "peach basketing" of earlier weeks had been only small stuff of little value. If we were to make major choices, the time was now.

This began a curious period in our relationship, for it represented the first time that each of us was in a position to think solely of his or her own interest. The division was perfectly agreeable, for we had witnessed family fights in our youth and had no overt desire to do the same ourselves. We had agreed much earlier in the summer that "There is enough here for all of us." Furthermore, neither of my cousins had lived in the house, and even my own days when I had spent weekends there with my parents were so far back in the past that I could barely remember them.

None of us, therefore, had any emotional attachment to any of its furnishings, which had in the past led to family squabbles over "Cousin Mary's tea set" or "Grandmother's dinner plates." For myself, it had often been the things that we had thrown out that I loved, the enormous hornet's nest that was mounted (happily without its tenants) in the hall, the bundles of lavender dried twenty-five years before and found in an upstairs bureau. In addition, there was the vase of bayberries picked in the summer and kept on the hall sideboard in winter, and that I had found that first day. Finally there was that last taste of Open Country buckwheat honey in the comb found in the same sideboard and already carried lovingly to my own home in Los Angeles.

And yet, a curious kind of competition between us emerged. More properly, an accelerated competition, for its beginnings were not discernable. Early in the summer, we had all enjoyed the process of discovery, the seemingly endless childhood Christmas atmosphere of finding all kinds of beautiful and sometimes valuable items among the trash that filled the house. Later, as the problem of disposal began to weigh heavily upon us, when the house became simply one huge contest between us and various antique dealers, none of us had the heart to want anything. At the same, all the talk of values, actual cash values, seemed to have an effect on us all and to stimulate one of the least attractive of human attributes—greed.

Until we settled on Parke-Bernet's suggested method of handling things, we had not taken much out of the house. Once we made our decision, there was no further need to delay. We began quietly enough, with linens—for we all recognized that these would have little sale value, whereas my cousins could use them.

This proved a severe disappointment, however. Though we had three closets full, much of the linen was old and worn. A lot of it was too worn for use and actually should have been thrown away thirty years before. We all had been accumulating rags in a corner of the dining room to sell to Mr. Rubino when we were all through, and a large percentage of the linens found their way there.

By coincidence, however, they were destined for better use. About this time, a friend of mine from New Jersey came to visit with her aunt, and the aunt asked for the old linens. She told us she volunteered at a church whose members folded disposable bed dressings for patients with cancer and other diseases that impaired their ability to control elimination. These linens, she said, were perfect for the purpose, soft and disposable. Would I give them to her?

I was delighted. It seemed appropriate somehow, because Cousin Margaret's sister had died in a downstairs bedroom of one of those illnesses, that those remnants should go to this worthy purpose. I was also able to pass on to this woman something else that gave me equal pleasure. Having spent much of the summer putting out birdseed in Cousin Margaret's bird feeder in a window of her garage apartment, I had run out of birdseed and, feeling that the little creatures should learn how to fend for themselves, I had bought no more. This same woman admired the bird feeder— she admitted that she had only a makeshift one outside her own kitchen window at home. Then and there, I took it down and gave it to her, reflecting that Cousin Margaret would be glad to think that her feeder would continue to give good service.

After going through the linens and agreeing to give those in the worst shape to my New Jersey friend, my cousins and I turned our attention to things of greater value. I did not foresee that any of us would choose very much. Katherine had a large house, but it was well furnished, and furthermore she had it on the market and was thinking of moving to smaller quarters. Lloyd and Louise had a four-room house that I gathered was, if anything, a little crowded. I, of course, would have to move anything I wanted three thousand miles, which sort of restricted my choices.

I had only picked out a set of the eighteenth-century Chinese export coffee cups with straight sides and deep saucers for myself. There were thirteen of them, and I had an additional seven on the West Coast, a set that I had always liked. They were simple in design, and I wanted to bring the set back together again, for the pattern was the same, and I strongly believed that they had originally belonged to the Remsens, common ancestors of mine and Cousin Margaret's who had once owned a house where the Manhattan side piers of the Brooklyn Bridge now stand. This was, however, the extent of my own choices.

About my cousins, however, I was wrong, dead wrong. All the talk of values and rarities must have penetrated their emotions more than I realized, for their desires were not as modest as mine.

We began making a list, walking from room to room and indicating items of our choice. Gradually, I watched my cousins' lists grow longer, and I began to perceive a *sub rosa* competition emerging between Katherine and Louise. Lloyd was horrified. He was, I think, torn between feeling that he'd have to move out of their house and sleep in the garage for lack of houseroom and fearing that he'd have to get a divorce. The air was laden with his complaints while his wife spelled out what she wanted to take away from Open Country.

For my part, I wanted nothing more than the cups and saucers, but it became clear that, on a cash basis, the two women wanted far more than I did. At first, I tried to persuade my cousins to have values set on the things they wanted to take so that they could pay me in cash for their share of the takings out of the proceeds of the house sale. I made a number of noises to this effect, but my words fell on oddly deaf ears. I met a kind of uncomprehending resistance that puzzled me deeply, for my ideas seemed reasonable and fair under the circumstances. To me at least.

Finally, I came to the inescapable conclusion that my cousins had fallen prey to the idea of a *freebie*. Without actually realizing that their share of the goods *per se* would reduce their cash share of the take, they were acting as if Open Country was some giant store where all the merchandise was free. Their resistance, I thought, was due to the fact that they did not *want* to know the cost of their choices. That would have taken the fun out of getting them for free!

The problem was compounded by the fact that, between the date on which we made our agreement with Parke-Bernet and the date of their arrival to make choices, my cousins, chiefly Katherine and Louise, seemed to grow more acquisitive. It was almost as if

Parke-Bernet were some sort of parent figure that would rap their knuckles if it knew how much they were taking.

Not only were they anxious to get their merchandise out of the house before Parke-Bernet's arrival, but the pace of their choices picked up day by day. After our initial tour of the house with our lists, they kept saying, "Oh, by the way, you know the little table in the upper hall? Would you mind ..."

In each case, the rest of us would reply, "Not at all."

Then, with a moment's thought, "I think I'll set it against Katherine's ..." this last to keep things equal.

It was almost as if a competition had set in to see who could do best. Fortunately, as we all had said, there *was* plenty to go around and there was always something to "set against" the latest acquisition.

Almost by common but unspoken agreement, nobody chose from among the things considered of real value, with one or two possible exceptions. I had made no secret of the value of my cups; Katherine had early set her heart on the Highboy that Rubenstein had admired; and Louise had long wanted the Duncan Pfyfe dining room chairs before they had been so identified. Except for those, however, the choices seemed to be limited to those things that were admired by antique dealers, but about which no special noises had been made.

Actually, this acceleration of choosing crystallized my thinking about something I had had in my mind for some time. Lloyd and Louise had been talking all summer about hoping to move from their small Long Island home to a place in Connecticut, and I had been joking with them about opening an antique shop and running it from the supplies at Open Country, with me and Katherine as silent partners.

Lloyd had shown little interest in the idea, but as the summer wore on, I became more interested myself. Why not, I wondered, do it myself? Late in the summer, a couple of friends came up for a visit, one of them a highly creative person with a flair for color and decoration, and the other the controller of a small company. We discussed the idea jokingly among ourselves, and presently it grew beyond the joke stage.

As my cousins' acquisitiveness grew, and I became increasingly aware of my need to protect my own interests, the idea of the shop became concrete, and Ander, Carey, and I agreed definitely to go into business. Therefore, I pitched in cheerfully in making choices, competing perfectly happily with my cousins, matching choice for choice.

The Eyesore came in for heavy use during this period, traveling every day or so to New York full of accumulated treasures for "Early Clutter," as we had named the new enterprise. By the time Parke-Bernet came to make their choices, our own were gone from the house, though, like my cousins, I avoided items that were plainly Parke-Bernet's province.

They brought a regular team with them, a specialist in china and glass, another in furniture, another in books, and so on. They went through the house like greased lightning, placing tags on everything they wanted, including a good selection of the dolls and dolls' furniture. We made arrangements with a local moving firm, and in a very few days, the prize pieces were gone, including the white jade bowl that we had treated so casually during the summer—and that brought $250 at auction, which was a surprise to us all. Once again, we turned our minds to the problem of the hundreds of remaining items and how to dispose of them.

All summer long, this problem had hung over our heads like a thundercloud. Cousin Margaret's instructions had been most specific. "No Auction shall be held on my property," the will read. We were all reasonably sure why the restriction had been put there. Cousin Margaret was a fiercely proud woman, and she would not have wanted the general public tramping through the ruins of her once-fine home. This sort of public display of the level to which the place had sunk would have been bitterly abhorrent to her.

Yet, what were we to do? We still had an enormous mass of

material to deal with. Moving it would be ruinously expensive, and, even if we did move it, where would we take it? Where would be find a building large enough to display the items to be auctioned off?

We even drove a mile or so down the road to another house, a great, gaunt terrifying ruin standing on top of a nearby hill. To get there, we drove up a winding, overgrown driveway until we rounded the final curve and the house loomed menacingly above us. It was pure Charles Addams, a three-story granite building with most of the windows gone or standing broken in their frames. Wisteria had claimed most of the port cochere and the front door stood half-open.

Inside, we found the building stripped; mantels, stair-rails, lighting fixtures gone; the library paneling and bookcases removed; the plumbing stripped from the bathrooms. It was desolation on a greater scale than Open Country because the house had been grander in its inception, a true country palace built for some industrial baron of the 1890s. For our purposes it was impossible, too dangerous, and lacked parking facilities or a decent way for our customers to get in or out.

We also discussed a device for holding the auction at Open Country, but not actually on the property. Cousin Margaret had not forbidden a *viewing* on the property, just the auction. She had sold most of the surrounding acreage and, if a survey map in her desk was accurate, the field beyond the vegetable garden was not hers. Therefore, we could hold the viewing in the house and have the things carried across the fence to a tent set up in the adjacent field for the sale.

Unfortunately, our reading of the map proved to be wrong, and that idea went out of the window. We finally decided to disobey the provisions of the will. The lawyer in New York simply would not be told about it, and if none of her local friends kicked up a fuss, it would be all right. We salved our consciences with the conclusion that Cousin Margaret had no idea what problems her prohibition created, and convinced ourselves that, any case, she was close with her money and would hate to see it wasted in unnecessary moving.

It was at this juncture that O. Rundle Gilbert came to see us one day. We had heard about him all summer, from Jordy Jack, from Tim Trace, from Parke-Bernet and from others. We had the impression that he was a "country auctioneer," who could manage an auction but who did not deal in high-priced goods such as ours.

We were wrong on both counts. Mr. Gilbert was an astute businessman who handled us with a frankness that made me wish that we had talked to him earlier in the summer. In the first place, he told us, though we had an enormous quantity of goods to sell, we did not have enough valuable things to build an auction around.

"The way to get a crowd," he said, "is to have some unusual or outstanding pieces to advertise. If there are only a few good pieces in a house, an auctioneer will sometimes "salt' the auction with a few additional good pieces to give the auction additional class. Right now, you have really nothing to build an auction around. What you should do, he added, is to hold a house sale."

He was kind enough not to voice the suspicion that he had been offered second pickings, as had been the case, and he left us wondering whether Parke-Bernet's advice had been advice or merely a sales pitch. If we had made a mistake there, it was not a very big one.

A house sale. The idea had been discussed several times, but not very specifically, and we wondered how to go about setting one up. It was Jordy who proposed a solution.

"Why don't you get in touch with Tim Trace?" he asked. "He runs heavy house sales, and very good ones too. You've got to do it fast," he added. "The season is almost over." I discussed the idea with my cousins, and they agreed. Louise was particularly delighted because she had been very impressed when she had met him several weeks before.

Tim came over to see us, estimated that he could get at least $3,500 for the remaining things in the house, and said that his fee would be 10 percent. My cousins and I agreed to let him do the job for us. We no longer had any idea about how correct his estimate might be, but we concluded that we would be selling directly to the general public, and that we ought to do fairly well.

We set a date two weeks away. I had to return to the West Coast briefly on business, but Tim said that nothing could be done by way of preparation until three or four days before the sale anyway, and we parted on that note.

I left a day or so later, promising to be back the Monday before the sale, which would be the following Saturday, a little over a week away. Much relieved, for all our problems seemed solved, and, having real confidence in Trace, I left for the coast.

A few days after I got home, I got a disturbing phone call from Lloyd.

"I say, old man, we've got problems."

"What kind of problems?"

"While you were gone, Katherine fired Trace." Lloyd also told me that she had brought a friend of hers up from Irvington named Paz (we never knew her last name), a woman who had once run an antique shop and who dabbled in interior decorating.

"Trace's estimate is nonsense," Lloyd told me she had said. "I can get at least ten thousand dollars for the things in the house. You're crazy to let that dreadful man do this to you. Why, I can get fifteen dollars apiece for these alone," she'd said, holding up a jet embroidered jacket from the 1890s that we had despaired of getting rid of.

As a result, Lloyd continued, Katherine had fired Tim summarily and retained Paz to do the job. Lloyd told me further that neither he nor Louise was happy about it, but they felt powerless faced with Katherine's forceful actions.

We were, it seemed, back in the soup again.

CHAPTER 9

I Guess I'll Just Have to Come Down a Nickel

When I arrived back in Open Country, things were in still worse shape. Louise was very annoyed. It seemed that Paz had set a price of five dollars apiece on four crystal and silver vegetable dishes that my friends in Early Clutter had estimated were worth at least $200. They had been checking out antique shops in New York since we had first discussed the idea of our shop. She'd then tried to buy them herself at that price to give away as a wedding present.

Louise, of course, had seen through the maneuver and was livid.

"I don't mind, Russell," she said to me after I got back. "If you get good prices when you are buying for the shop. In the first place, you're family, and in the second place you've done so much, what with bringing your friends and all to help that you deserve it. Anyway, I know you have to think of your markup. But that woman and Katherine were just out to cheat us!"

As I listened to her, I had a flashback to my visit with Mr. Quinn in his office before I returned to Open Country. He had swung his chair around and pulled a book from the bookcase behind his back.

"Henry Seidel Canby," he had said. *"Home in the Nineties."* He'd riffled through the pages looking for the passage he wanted and he'd begun again, "The slow crushing of a family by its home ... until in a final scene, with depleted capital or broken health, the hollow shell of the home collapsed on a ruined estate and fiercely quarreling heirs."

I was chilled by the reminder. I had known Lloyd and Katherine since I was a child and had met Louise in my pre-adolescence. I had loved all three of them, and we four had by then agonized over the house and its contents for almost three months. Were we condemned to duplicate the quotation Mr. Quinn had read to me at our meeting in June? I found it a troubling thought and resolved to play the peacemaker as best I could.

Aside from that, we had a serious problem facing us. It was now September 24, and we were due to have the sale on the September 29. It was getting cold, and there was no heat in the Big House; we did not know what condition the furnaces were in or whether it would be wise even to light them after all those years. We could expect the first frost any day, if it had not already occurred while I was in Los Angeles. We could not afford to wait any longer.

When I arrived, Lloyd and Louise picked me up at the airport and drove me over to Katherine's for a conference. I outlined my conclusions with them while we were on our way. It was a bad bargain, I said, but I saw no other choice than to let Paz do it.

Our conference with Katherine and Paz was not comfortable. Paz, it seemed, had previously said that she was angry about Louise's alleged ill treatment of her, but she was willing to negotiate with me to patch things up. Louise told me that she had bristled at her effrontery but had held her tongue, and on that note we arrived at Paz's house.

Paz's house was lush. There was no other word to describe it. Large, with white wall-to-wall carpeting, gilt and crystal sconces all over the place, Louis-something furniture, marble fireplaces, the works. It was the stylish house of an interior decorator. As for

Paz herself, she wore stylish black pants and a gold-embroidered jacket and had short red hair, though I could not tell whether it was natural or enhanced. Paz herself looked vaguely familiar to me, but I could not quite tell why. To my acute distress, all of her conversation was directed at me. Plainly, she regarded me as the central control force to reckon with.

Without referring directly to her dispute with Louise, she paid me the compliment of saying that she understood that I had a wide knowledge of antique prices and told me that she would be willing to continue work if I would agree to act as price arbiter.

I did not like the position she put me in because my interests were now divided between myself as seller of the goods and also linked to my partners in Early Clutter as prospective buyers at the sale. I outlined this difficulty to the group, but I added that I would be willing to accept the responsibility if they would trust me to be fair in my dealings with both sides. Paz said that she was sure she could work with me on that basis, and my cousins agreed that they could trust me.

I was personally unhappy with the arrangement because I knew I did not have the knowledge that I was credited with, but I also knew that we were in a bad position, and I was determined to make the best of it and deal with whatever happened as best I might.

First of all was the problem of newspaper advertising. It was now Tuesday, and I knew from my own newspaper experience that most weeklies close their ad columns either Tuesday afternoon or Wednesday morning at the latest. The group showed little interest in the matter, but I forced them to help draft an advertisement for the house sale.

Once that matter was settled, Lloyd, Louise, and I left for Open Country. On the way, we discussed the outcome of the meeting. I told them that I saw that I had no choice but to act as arbiter, however uncomfortable I would feel in that role.

"I guess you're right," Louise admitted during the drive. "We should never have allowed Katherine to get away with it. But, since we have, we're stuck. I must admit that she has done a magnificent job of setting the place up. It really looks beautiful. Just wait until you see."

As soon as I got back to the apartment, I went straight to the telephone to arrange for ads in local papers within a radius of forty miles of Open Country. It was lucky I did so, for I made the deadline of the most important one by just fifteen minutes; I was late for another, but I managed to talk the woman on the phone into accepting the ad anyway.

This done, Lloyd, Louise, and I walked over to the house. It was a magnificent fall day, and, in the ten days since I was there last, the leaves had begun to turn. The great, gloomy maples shading the driveway and the house were now a symphony of red and yellow, and their reflected light gave the house a sense of light and air that it had not had all summer.

Compared with its dejected air earlier, Open Country looked magnificent. Paz had laid rugs, draped curtains, and arranged furniture around the main hall as well as in the living and dining rooms. Candlesticks, bric-a-brac, and fans were laid about attractively on tables and fireplace mantels, and the house nearly had a lived-in look. An outsider would, I suppose, have been appalled at the wallpaper that still hung in strips from the walls amid the fallen plaster, but, to one who had lived all summer with the dingy, unkempt house, it looked magnificent.

Louise had brought up folding church-supper tables to lay things on, and the ground-floor bedroom where Cousin Catherine had died had been established as the one-dollar room; the servants' dining room as the twenty-five-cent room—anything in those two rooms would be available at its single price. In this way, we hoped to get rid of a lot of items that might be difficult to sell otherwise, because people love to rummage for bargains in that type of atmosphere.

We seemed to have made a good start, and I felt very much heartened by what I saw. If Paz really did know pricing, and this was crucial, we were set for a good sale. I did not think she could get anywhere near $10,000, but, if she could, more power to her. She had promised to call a number of her better-heeled customers and acquaintances, and if we could sell to them, all well and good.

Paz was supposed to come up the next day, Wednesday, to start pricing, and I looked forward to her appearance. Lloyd and Louise went home, and I retired in good spirits in Cousin Margaret's apartment.

Next day, no Paz. Katherine did not appear, but she phoned to say that Paz had a dental appointment, but that she would be up on Thursday. For me, this was cutting it a little close, but Lloyd and Louise agreed, but we were in no position to argue.

Paz came up the next day, but not until early afternoon. She brought a friend with her, and they concentrated on laying out the dresses that the museum people had not taken. She called it "Madame LaZonga's Salon," which would have surprised Cousin Margaret to no end, since it was her bedroom that was being used. As elsewhere in the house, Paz did a very good job of laying things out attractively. Her friend dickered with me over a few of the curtains, and Paz herself bought a couple of pairs of portieres. But beyond that, no pricing was accomplished. As I looked about the vast expanse of things to be priced, I did not see how we were going to get it all done in time.

Paz's friend had driven her up and had to leave early, and Paz prevailed on me to drive her back home that night. She was a charming companion, and, for all that I was both annoyed and worried, I thoroughly enjoyed the trip down in the Eyesore. She invited me to meet her husband and a friend of hers and to have dinner with them.

As soon as I entered her living room, I knew why she had looked vaguely familiar when we first met. Paz herself had not always been the redhead she was that night, but a dark brunette. Her friend, seated on the couch, wore a pair of orange-red patent leather high-heeled shoes, and, though she seemed to be living in the house, had an orange-red bag of the same material beside her. When I looked at Paz in her black shirt and black sweater, and looked down at her feet, which seemed the same size as her friend's, I remembered.

Some weeks before, I had been loading the last of Cousin Margaret's hothouse plants into the Eyesore so that I could take them over to Jordy, who had a well-equipped hothouse of his own. I had noticed lights in the house and a car parked outside the kitchen door. It was already deep dusk, and I could think of nothing but thieves, and I had hot-footed my way down the drive and burst into the house.

I must have looked a sight, my fists at the ready, wearing tattered sneakers and blue jeans and a faded work shirt, and I was met in the big hall by a faintly amused, distinguished-looking bald man in a business suit. He introduced himself as George Gray, said he was a friend of Katherine's, and said that they were supposed to meet her there.

Naturally, I had cooled down immediately and introduced myself. As we stood chatting, someone had come down the stairs, a woman with dark brunette hair, wearing a black skirt and a black cashmere sweater, and carrying a small flashlight. She was walking stocking-footed and did not seem too sober. I then noticed that Gray was carrying a pair of orange-red patent leather high-heeled shoes and a large purse of the same color and material in his hands.

Gray had introduced her as his sister, and she repeated the same story that he had handed me. They expressed disappointment in missing Katherine (who was not expected that evening), and left. I asked Katherine about them the next time I saw her. She denied having sent any friends to the house and acted mystified by the whole affair. I dismissed the incident from my mind as just another Open Country mystery until that night in Paz's house.

Looking at the two of them on the sofa, I was dead sure that Paz had been the woman on the stairs, and she had simply been too drunk then to recognize me when she saw me later, in her house dressed in civilized clothing. I already knew enough about her to know that she had neither brothers nor sisters and, as I sat looking at her and the man she said was her husband, who was bald, I wondered just what games she was playing, and with whom. I had met one of the two women that night, but in the dim light of the hall I was not sure which, though I believed it to have been Paz.

I didn't care who the man was, but I wondered whether Katherine had sent her up to look the place over, or whether she had done it on her own after hearing Katherine's tales about our findings. I suspected the former because Open Country was not that easy to find unless one had meticulous directions.

It was not a pleasant evening. Paz's friend was in the midst of a messy divorce, and the two women got drunk. Paz produced an excellent dinner, and I enjoyed her husband's company when the conversation was not dominated by the two women discussing their respective divorces, but I breathed a sigh of relief when I finally left the house.

The next day, Friday, was no more satisfactory than Thursday had been. Paz came up in the late morning with a friend who bought a few things. Jordy was there, and under his direction I upgraded some of the prices of the china the friend wanted to buy, which cost us a few sales and did not please Paz. They later sold, however, at the same prices that Jordy had placed on them, which vindicated my judgment. Paz left early with almost no pricing done, promising to be back first thing in the morning. This time, she was as good as her word. She was there at 9:00 a.m. and began energetically to place prices on things. My partners were there too, for I had established with Paz and my cousins at the first interview with Paz that family had the first right to buy before Paz and after pricing.

Paz's pricing was simply crazy. There is no other word to describe it. At first, she kept asking advice of anyone near her. "Louise," she would say, holding up something, "what do you think this is worth? Do you think we could get five dollars for it?"

Depending on whether or not Louise, or whoever it was, agreed, that would be the price. I was mad clear through, for not only had she postponed this to the last minute, but she was demonstrating clearly that she did not know what she was talking about. Finally, my temper snapped.

"Paz," I finally yelled from the balcony above the entrance hall, "we hired you because you said you knew how to price antiques. Now quit asking other people's advice and do it!"

It was rude, but justified, and after that she did her pricing on her own. Checking her prices as I went around, I could find no pattern to her thinking at all. A few prices seemed to be in the right ballpark, but this apparently only by chance, for most of her prices for them were either too high or too low.

Overhearing her instructing people to put things in the one-dollar and twenty-five-cent rooms, I decided to check these as well. What I saw surprised me even more. Many of the items *did* deserve to be there, but, in addition there were a number of glaring errors, as for example a fine wrought-iron hanging lantern in the one-dollar room.

My patience snapped and, encouraged by Lloyd and Louise, I decided that, since things had gotten completely out of hand I decided that I would cease looking out for Hunter-Robertson-Wheeler and start looking out for Russell Hunter and his own partners.

Since my partners were there to buy and my cousins apparently had no desire to buy, I told Ander and Carey to go around and buy whatever had an unreasonably low price on it. Paz was still pricing, and I finally had to stand at her elbow to force her to keep at it as the day progressed, my partners scurried around like little beavers putting their red stickers on whatever was sharply underpriced and carrying things outside after reporting the item(s) and the price(s) to Louise, who was our treasurer. Paz was visibly annoyed at this tactic, for she evidently wanted some leisure to shop for herself after she had underpriced the things she wanted. Since, however, I had claimed the right for the family to shop first, I saw no reason to let her slack off on her work.

Lloyd was apparently aware of what was going on, and he apparently approved, for, late in the afternoon, he came up to Ander and Carey with a small cardboard box in his hand.

"Here," he said. "I found this in some trash that Paz threw out. I think you'd like to have it." When they had opened it, they found a complete set of paper cutout dolls and dolls' clothing from the eighties, the duplicate of a set given to the Museum of the City of New York a few weeks earlier, and published in *LOOK* magazine!

At the end of the day, we were exhausted. Fully one-third of the pricing had yet to be done, but Paz said she had to go home. It was obvious to me that we would not finish that day, and I dreaded the dawn of the next day in our unprepared state. Paz, who had been brought up by a friend once again, was without a car, and she prevailed on Louise to drive her back home.

The Jacks had invited me to dinner, and I drove over to their house. Bennet had been at Open Country earlier that day, and had aroused Paz's ire by buying from under her nose a black velvet skirt from the 1890s that she, and Paz as well probably, planned to have made over into a dinner dress. Grateful as I was to Bennet and Jordy for their help and kindness during the summer, I had forced Paz to put a price on it, and the dress went to Bennet.

Jordy had been over at the same time, and the three of us were gloomily discussing our chances the next day, when the phone rang. It was Louise, and she asked for me.

"Paz quit," were her first words.

"What? The day before the sale?" was all I think of to say.

"Yes." Louise said. And then she chuckled. "It's not so funny, Russell, but do you know what she said? 'That man is impossible. I cannot work with him another minute. Just let me have my ten percent of the sales made so far. I'm not coming back.'"

"I'm sorry I caused this."

"That's all right. You did all you could do. The question is, now what do we do? Run it ourselves?"

That was clearly impossible. If Paz knew little, we knew even less., and I foresaw complete ruin the next day if something was not done.

"Tell you what I'll do, if you and Lloyd agree. I'll phone Tim Trace and ask him to help us. I have no right to do it, and he has every reason to turn us down cold. but I'll try. Is that all right with you?"

"Of course, Russell." I could hear her take the phone away from her mouth to call to Lloyd. "Russell wants us to call Tim Trace. That's all right, isn't it?"

In the distance, I heard Lloyd's calm voice. "By all means."

"Fine," I said, "I'll call him right now and get back to you later."

Just to cover all the bases, I called Katherine to let her know that we were doing. She had not been at Open Country the past two days, but I still felt I owed her that courtesy. She was not home, and I was glad. My conscience was clear, and I could go ahead with what had to be done.

Mentally on my knees, I called Tim Trace. "Tim," I said, "we're in a spot. That woman my cousin Katherine hired while I was gone has quit on us. And the sale is tomorrow. Are you still free to run the sale for us?"

To my amazement, Tim said he would and agreed to be with us the next morning at eight o'clock. I was so overjoyed to just to get him that I neglected to ask what he would charge. Under the circumstances, nothing was as important as getting him.

I called back Lloyd and Louise and gave them the good news, and they were as relieved as I. I also told them that I had tried to call Katherine but that she was out.

We agreed that we should notify her of what we had done and also close the door firmly in Paz's face in case she tried to return the next morning to patch things up. It occurred that she might be playing games with us and had no intention of quitting.

It was a dirty trick, but I decided to contact both women by overnight telegraph so that the message would not be delivered to them until the next morning, at which point they could do nothing. Paz, I knew from my one evening there, was likely to be tight that evening, and I had learned weeks before that Katherine began drinking about five o'clock and could not talk business after six. Too tight. I figured both women probably got up with hangovers in the morning, and if I was to drop bad news in their lap, early morning was the time to do it. Furthermore, by the time they got the telegrams the sale would already be in process.

To Katherine, I sent the following over my signature as well as Lloyd's and Louise's, after they had okayed it.

"Paz Thompson quit this afternoon, and we are accepting her resignation. Have hired Tim Trace to run the sale for us tomorrow."

To Paz, I sent the following: "We accept your resignation and will be happy to pay you ten percent of all sales to date. Thank you for your good work."

When Katherine heard about it, she was furious. She called the next day at about nine thirty, after the sale had been in progress for about an hour and a half. What seemed to enrage her as much as anything else was the fact that I had not asked Tim Trace what his fee would be. Perhaps that had been unwise, but I figured him to be a fair man, and I had faith that his services would not come unreasonably high. I was right. He charged us 10 percent, which is what he had originally asked for.

"I won't pay a penny of his commission," Katherine raged to me on the phone.

"Very well, cousin," I said coldly, *I* will pay every penny of it. All right, cousin?"

"All right," she said bitterly. "Good-bye." She slammed down the phone with so much force that I jumped when I heard it hit the cradle on her side before it had even cut off the connection.

Lloyd and Louise were very generous about the incident. "We can't let you do that, Russell," they said. "We'll pay half of it. It's not fair for you to pay it all."

I was grateful, said so, and accepted their kind offer. Katherine later relented and agreed to pay her fair share, but she but I never spoke to each other again.

She called no more, neither on the day of the sale nor the next. Two days later, she called Lloyd, still in a rage, and that most patient man gave her a reading out "Such as I have not heard him deliver in the thirty years I have known him," Louise told me later.

Katherine had driven up that afternoon ostensibly to do some buying on her own, but, finding nothing left that she liked, she had stalked about the house for about fifteen minutes like an angry duchess, missing only a lorgnette, and left. I did not see her again, and, after the telephone call, it was some time before she and Lloyd spoke to each other again.

On the evening before the sale, having persuaded Tim Trace to rescue us the next day, I returned to a very pleasant dinner with Bennet and Jordy. Tomorrow would be rough, we agreed, but we had a good chance of selling well with Trace around to protect us from the dealers we were sure would be there to buy in bulk. When Ander, Carey, and I returned to Cousin Margaret's little apartment, we were in good spirits.

Whistling wind and rattling shutters woke us rudely before daylight. There were other sounds as well, the wet sounds of heavy rain on the roof of Cousin Margaret's little apartment. We were plainly faced with one of the equinoctial storms for which that part of the country is famous in late September.

"What's that?"

"Rain."

"Oh hell. The parking area will be a swamp."

"And the house will be like an iceberg. And dark as a tomb. As if the maples did not cut out enough light from overhead, we gotta have clouds and rain to make it even darker."

I reached over and switched on the light and found that the wet sounds of rain from outside seemed to accentuate the bareness of Cousin Margaret's little apartment. Since we had taken all the furniture over to the Big House the day before, the living room was bare. The only things left in the room were the telephone, one bridge lamp, and the three mattresses on which we had made our beds.

As Ander raised himself sleepily on one elbow, Carey stirred slightly in his tangle of blankets and asked grumpily, "What time is it?"

"Five."

"a.m.?"

"Yes, you idiot."

"What's that?"

"Rain."

"Oh, God! Coffee!"

This abrupt change in the weather left us with a pot full of problems. To begin with, even in the pre-dawn darkness I could see that the driveway was a running river of water, which meant that the ground around us was soggy. It would be impossible to use the vegetable garden as a parking lot, which we had planned to do.

It also meant that the house would be cold, damp, and dark. Much of the ground floor had been gloomy all summer because of the wisteria growing over the porches, and they had become reasonably light only when the leaves began to turn to their fall colors of red and yellow. It was still gloomy in the house, however, and most of the wall fixtures in the house were either too dim to provide any effective lighting or did not work at all.

Not the least of our problems was the cold. The house was just warm enough during the day with the sun on it and with a warm breeze blowing through the open doors and windows, but after a night of cool weather it was cool again, and this morning it would be glacial.

As soon as it was daylight, we slopped over to the Big House. The rooms were so cold we could see our own breath.

"Now what do we do? If anyone is fool enough to come out in this weather, we'll have to chip the ice off of them to get their money. Furnace work?"

"Hasn't been used for more than twenty years," I replied, thinking of my little cousin trying to stay warm in her bedroom above the laundry room in the servants' wing. "We'll have to build fires in the fireplaces. At least things will look more cheerful. We'll get candles and stick them in the wall brackets where the lights won't work. That'll make some light in those rooms."

"Where do we get wood?"

"From the porches. Whoever buys this place will have to tear them down. There are some dry crates by the front door, and once we get them going, we can tear the loose bits off the outside of the porches. Even if they're wet they'll burn once the fire is started."

"Do the chimneys work or are they clogged?" This from Ander, who had a practical mind.

"They used to have fires in the living room when I was a kid. The hall fireplace doesn't look as if it has ever been used, but the dining room one is black with use. I'll check the flues when there is more light outside."

"But that will mean climbing all over the roof in the rain."

"Can you think of another way?"

"No."

When the fires had been laid, I scrambled out an attic skylight to look for loose bricks, birds' nests or other obstructions inside the chimneys. It was still pouring down rain, and the roof shingles were slippery with wet lichen. I had given Ander a flashlight, and he shone the flashlight on each fireplace in turn. That light enabled me to check each chimney for obstructions.

Sitting astride the ridgepole of the dining room wing, I looked down and saw that the rain had turned the drive into a river. Even the ruts were hidden by the torrent of muddy water pouring down the road outside.

Ander's flashlight shone strong and clear up each chimney. I found, indeed, that the hall fireplace had never been used. It had been beautifully made, lined all the way up with yellow firebrick, but it was clean, untouched by soot.

I was soaking wet when I was through, and, as I prepared to scramble down through the skylight, I saw something else at the end of the driveway. A car was turning off the main road and starting to pick its way up the drive. Customers, and the advertised starting time more than an hour away! Hastily, I scrambled back over the roofs and down to the big hall to warn the others.

"Chimneys work?" Ander asked eagerly.

"Yeah, you can light the fires. They're fine. The hall chimney hasn't been used in the seventy years since it was put up. Must be some sort of a record. The flue is spotless. And, oh yes we've got customers arriving. I just saw them turning into the driveway when I was on the roof."

When I got downstairs, I found all of the fires lit and drawing well. Ander had collected dry wood from the cellar and was stripping rotten bits from the porches and elsewhere. These, along with the wisteria branches, served us all day and kept the house reasonably warm until the late afternoon.

Bennet and Jordy phoned early and offered to bring a store of candles for the lightless rooms, and we accepted gratefully. When Jordy arrived, he had an ax in his hands. "I'm hoping to operate on the wisteria outside the living room windows. We've got to get some light in there." Presently, the sound of chopping and tearing could be heard from the area of Cousin Margaret's garden, and, when he was through, there were wisteria trunks all over the lawn outside.

In the meantime, I placed candles in the wall brackets in which the electricity didn't work. Bennet, who liked bright colors, had brought a complete assortment of them—black, gold, red, orange—and they imparted a feeling of déclassé elegance to the rooms as they flickered and dripped all day long.

My cousins had not been idle either. Louise had made coffee, and their daughter, Mimi, had set them up in a cashier's table near the hall fireplace where they would be warm. Lloyd had put up signs and strung ropes to keep people from walking on dangerous parts of the porch, and he and his son, Stephen, tried to figure out how to arrange the parking. The two men worked like beavers all day at this, trying to keep the drive clear, helping customers out to their cars with their purchases, and helping cars that got mired in the goo alongside the driveway.

Tim Trace and his wife arrived early, though not before that first car had picked its way up the driveway, and he had been taking stock of the situation. Mrs. Trace was an expert in materials, and it was agreed that she would handle the dresses, the curtains, and other similar materials, while he handled all other sales. By the time our first customers walked into the house, we were at least half-ready to receive them.

All pricing, he told us all, was to be cleared through him, and we watched fascinated throughout the day as he did an extraordinary job, pricing swiftly, bargaining harshly with professionals, more kindly with the general public, and most gently with children who came to him with the smallest items.

"Don't give me that," he snapped at a dealer with a picture frame in his hand. "That gilt is perfectly good. That's dirt, and you know it. My price stands."

To a little girl a few minutes later, "Well, my dear, since all you have is twenty-five cents, I guess I'll just have to come down a nickel. Go and tell the lady by the cash box that Mr. Trace said you could have it for twenty-five cents."

Louise and Mimi were snowed in with people standing in line saying "Mr. Trace says …" and handing over their money. Mimi, who worked for a large department store on Long Island, stood out in sharp contrast to her mother. She was dressed in style, her hair platinum blonde and her face carefully made-up. Looking at Louise, who never wore makeup, her glasses now continually on her nose, her eyeglass in constant use as she identified china for purchasers—"Yes, it's Dresden. See the crossed swords on the back? And, with magnifying glass to her eye, "Now, how much did Mr. Trace say it was worth?" Then, as the money was handed over, "I hope you enjoy it." It did not seem possible that they were mother and daughter.

For me, it was a day of stoking fires and running errands. Little by little, the wisteria trunks that Jordy had chopped down disappeared up the fireplaces that we kept burning all day, as the did scrap lumber that had fallen from the porches around the house. By the end of the day, I had been reduced to ripping up pieces of the porch floor to keep the fires burning. Much to my surprise, however, the house remained warm. The great hall fireplace became hot enough, in fact, that Louise and her daughter had to leave their place by the fire and move their cash box to the middle of the floor.

The customers we had seen arriving early were an unprepossessing couple, the man in a shapeless suit and rumpled overcoat, the woman in heavy shoes, a country skirt, and a man's raincoat. First, we watched eagerly as they meandered around the house looking at things, but we soon forgot them as the pace of arrivals picked up and the house filled with people. We were a little surprised to learn later that they'd bought more than $500 worth of merchandise for their fashionable antique shop in New Canaan.

By the time of the official opening of the sale, the house was full to the rafters, and it stayed crowded until nightfall. We practically had to shove the last customers out the door, snatching their money from them as we did so.

We lost count of the number of cars that came, got stuck in the mud, and finally left loaded with purchases. They swarmed all over the house like locusts, clutching at things like shoppers at a Macy's sale. They pried into everything—closets, drawers, the cellar, the attic. They even got into Cousin Margaret's tenants' garage and removed a sixty-dollar set of tools without bothering to pay for them, something we had to pay for.

Everything in the house seemed to have a prospective customer. The remaining dolls were snapped up by collectors, the crocks that had sat dispiritedly in the kitchen were sold to other collectors, as were the glass insulators from telephone poles that had also sat in the kitchen—this time they were in the window where they would catch the light and attract customers. There was a busy market for curtains, for quilts, even for the bundles of Victorian women's underclothing that crowded the sewing room upstairs.

The Big House was a madhouse, like some giant anthill full of people wandering aimlessly about, their arms full of their purchases. There was a customer for everything in the house, even for the old dresses and petticoats that we had been unable to donate to a museum. Late in the afternoon, I passed a woman carrying a bundle of Aunt Annie's bustled petticoats and full, lace-edged bloomers from the eighties. Since Cousin Margaret's mother had tipped the scales at more than two hundred pounds when she'd died in 1923, I wondered what the woman wanted with them, but by that time I was too tired to have the energy to ask.

They were so much like acquisitive chipmunks, that we, who had systematically unpacked the house with great care during the previous three months, actually found ourselves selling things we had actually never seen.

My partners had been buying as well. Having gobbled up Paz's "bargains" the day before, they now turned their attention to the things which she had overlooked. Tim was a little kinder to them than to the other dealers who came for the sale, and, as a result, Early Clutter got some real bargains.

Through it all, Tim moved calmly, surrounded constantly by a group of customers wanting to know prices. He reminded me of my cousin Margaret, pan of chickenfeed in hand, surrounded by clucking chickens in one of the chicken runs. Cousin Margaret would have hated the idea of the general public traipsing through her beloved home, and she'd have bristled at the impious handling of her ancestors' belongings and clothing, but the job was close to done, and we were able to sag with relief.

The only fly in the ointment, of course, was Katherine. Lloyd withheld criticism, save for remarking that she should have been there to help, but Mimi was outspoken in her criticism of her Aunt Katherine. For myself, I thought it a shame that the summer should end on such a note, but fortunately family bitterness could do no more harm. The majority of the things in the house were gone, and not even a bitter Katherine could claim that Louise's accounting would not be accurate. We were fortunate, I reflected, that Katherine's cooperation had lasted as long as it did, given the contrast in our personalities.

Toward the late afternoon, the pace began to slow a little, and, as the evening shadows began to take over the Big House, we became suddenly aware that the house was beginning to seem almost empty, though there remained a lot of unsold things. The bulk of the job was over, however, and it only remained for the latecomers to pick over what was left. By day's end, however, we had raked in more than $4,000, almost twice what we had hoped to get for the entire contents.

The Jacks invited us over for a victory supper. Tim Trace and his wife, plainly exhausted, elected to return to their home in Peekskill, but the rest of us accepted gratefully. Tim said that we would stay "open" for a day or two longer, and that he would return the next day. On this note, we parted.

Ironically enough, the next day was as gorgeous as the previous day had been miserable, and the weather remained that way for the balance of my stay. Each day, the leaves turned a little brighter, and each day more of them fell from the maples for their winter of sleep, letting more light into the house.

We set up shop early the next day. Lloyd and I busied ourselves with bringing down unsold items from the second floor and stacking them on the tables in the dining room and another downstairs bedroom. One of my partners had returned to work in New York, but the other spent his time packing the Eyesore and trucking our purchases into New York. I made one or two trips with him and found it strange to see familiar items stacked and packed in boxes in the basement of the store they had rented while awaiting the sale. To my partners, the items were desirable merchandise on which they hoped to build a successful business. To me, they were something more and carried with them to New York something of Open Country and my own childhood that tugged painfully at my memory.

I saw again the old Victrola with the wooden horn on which I had heard my first music, the green teapot from which Cousin Margaret had poured countless cups of tea on the porch outside the living room, the container that used to hold bayberry branches in the fall and winter. There were also things of more recent, but still poignant, memory—the vegetable dishes found in the icehouse barrels and fought over by Paz and Louise, the sherry glasses that I had seen when I first opened the big sideboard in the dining room the June before. Each trip I took to New York brought back further memories for me, and each departure from New York brought me an additional painful twinge.

The pace of sales those last few days was leisurely. Monday, a few men came with their wives, men who had evidently been working on Sunday, but they did little buying, and their wives bargained carefully. It was clearly not the same moneyed crowd that had been there the previous day.

For the most part, Tim sat by the fire in the big hall, setting prices from time to time and talking with Louise and whichever of us happened to be present about past sales he had run. It came, he said, to a grand total of 216, including Open Country. He enjoyed sales, he said, and I had a sneaking suspicion that his acceptance of my Saturday night plea was not so much that he wanted to help us as it was that a sale under those circumstances was a challenge to him. Whatever the reason, we owed him a deep debt of gratitude, and said so time and again.

One customer in particular piqued Tim's interest. His name was Rocky, and he was an antique dealer from Stamford. A pack rat, Tim said, on a grand scale. He had been there the day before with his wife, and she had restrained his buying. "He'll be back without her," Tim prophesied, and he was right.

Rocky came in the middle of Monday morning and asked if he could look around. Trace smiled broadly and told him to go ahead, whereupon Rocky disappeared. We saw him from time to time in the cellar, in the attic, and rummaging about in the barns outside. He came up with, and paid cash for, things we'd never dreamed we could sell: an old icebox from the butler's pantry, a fishing tackle box without any tackle, odd bits of bridle, assorted bottles and jars, a beat-up bookcase from the attic. He even purchased the enormous sideboard from the dining room that I had looked into my first day at Open Country the previous June and that had not sold.

"I knew we'd do well when he came back," Tim told us. "He has several barns full of things he'll never sell. He can't resist this kind of thing. He always comes around after a sale and leaves with the same kind of tangle of oddments."

By Tuesday, we were all but through. Trace brought in a junk dealer he knew who gave us a price on the wretched, unsalable remains of china and glass and what few pieces of furniture remained. Louise came up the next day, but only to make arrangements for the final accounting. The barn was still full of wood from the Newtown House, of course, and Lloyd said he would try to sell it for us, but nothing else was left. The apartment was cleaned out, the plants in the greenhouse given away, the house stripped of everything of value. We had written *finis* to an era, disposed of the usable and useless *errata* of several lifetimes. Open Country was over.

Only the Eyesore was left. I had promised to let Katherine's son,

Bill, have it, and perhaps as a peace offering I decided to give it to him. I was not sure how to handle it, and Louise said she would be happy to deal with it for me. They later told me that he had a lot of fun with it, which somewhat took the sting out of my difficulties with his mother.

CHAPTER 10

It Was Not the Ruin ...

The following day, I was due to leave in the evening for the West Coast and, since I was alone, I walked over to the Big House feeling somewhat lost.

As I looked about the house after the last day of the sale, I realized that I had yet one more job to do for my little cousin. If she would have been mortified by the thought of the general public invading her once-proud home for a house sale, she would have been equally so at the thought of the new owner of Open Country coming in to find the wretched leavings of our sale. The house was bare of furniture, but littered with wrappings, scraps of unsold clothing, unsalable remnants of material, broken picture frames, and other flotsam that even the most penny-pinching buyers had judged valueless or irreparable.

I took a large push broom and, beginning in Cousin Margaret's bedroom, swept out each closet, each room, each hall, sweeping my way toward the stairs leading down to the entrance hall. Two or three times, the staircase became so full of debris that I had to stop and clear it, piling the accumulation in the big hall fireplace, where I set it ablaze. I went through each floor, each wing, in the same fashion, leaving behind only dust and barren rooms.

Sweeping and burning was almost a full day's job, and when I was through, I was filthy, but the house was neat. Late in the afternoon, Bennet and Jordy came over to drive me to my plane for the West Coast, and together we loaded my suitcases into their car for the trip to Idlewild Airport (now John F. Kennedy International Airport).

Once the car was loaded, I excused myself and returned to the house for a final, solitary, personal farewell. The giant maples surrounding the house were still brilliant with shades of crimson and gold in the bright October sunlight, but in the valley below the house, the trees had already, in the last few days, begun to lose their leaves and there were only a few bright spots in the gray landscape of the winter-to-be.

As I walked in the wide front door for the last time, I saw that the day's pyre was still smoldering gently on the hall hearth. I walked over to sweep a few scraps of embroidered linen into the coals before taking a final tour of the house.

As I turned to walk toward the living room, the full weight of our summer's burden struck me like a thunderbolt, and I started to weep. As I walked through the deserted and empty rooms, the tears flowed from some limitless source within me, and my final sight of Open Country was blurred by tears as I heard my sobs echoing through the emptiness of the old house.

Suddenly, it was not the ruin of Open Country that I was saying farewell to, but the warm and vibrant home I remembered from my childhood. Here was the living room, where we sat on cool evenings, my cousins, my parents, and I, in front of a warm fire. Here—the bedroom where I heard the first music I remember, a scratched recording of the Magic Fire Music from *Die Walküre* played on that windup Victrola with the enormous horn that was now in Early Clutter. And here, the corner of the porch where we used to have tea while admiring Cousin Margaret's flower garden, as well as the syringa bush whose perfume had come back to me with double force during my first days in the army.

The house was again filled with the August smell of spiced peaches being preserved in the kitchen under Cousin Catherine's watchful eye and the flower room perfumed by the September smell of English lavender drying for sachets.

As I stepped out of the living room and into the garden, the acrid odor of boxwood struck my nostrils, the only tangible remnant of all I remembered. The rest was gone, the life passed from existence into memory, the gardens into jungle, the furnishings escaped from years of dead storage into the warmth of others' homes, where they might once again provide a background for family life.

Hours later, as I winged my way westward, I felt as though an enormous weight had been lifted off me. The job was done, the huge accumulation of years had been disposed of, and my life could return to what it had been before Cousin Margaret had died. The reins of my West Coast life awaited me in Los Angeles. I had but to pick them up and go forward as before.

I was wrong, however. When I returned to my well-furnished small home on the West Coast, I found myself questioning my own belongings, the furniture, china, silver, and glass that I had inherited from my parents, as well as the Chinese export cups that I had brought from Open Country and whose packing still carrying with them the ghost of the odor of the decay at Open Country. I found myself suffering from something like a hangover, and it was a long time before I could put my own modest belongings in their proper place in my mind and heart.

My main task was to divorce them from all of the memories I had of my childhood at Open Country and of that sometimes heartbreaking summer that I had spent saying good-bye both to Cousin Margy and to the contents of Open Country. At first, I felt repulsed by my own possessions because they reminded me of that other world. Shortly, I realized that they lay not in my past but in my present and were thus separate from that particular past I had left on the East Coast.

Finally, I had to accept that we had done the best we could in finding new homes for Cousin Margaret's treasures and hope that she would have been pleased with what we did and how we did it.

Russell Hunter served in World War II, where he earned three battle stars in the European Theater of Operations (ETO) and then entered Harvard College, where he received his BA Cum Laude in 1950. He later earned a doctorate from UCLA and then taught graduate courses for almost thirty years. He currently lives in California.